The Angel of Christmas Alley

Lynette Rees

Contents

Chapter One

'Hurry up!' Pa shouted as he cast his daughter a beady-eyed stare. At twelve years old, Angeline Barker could hardly take another step. Her feet felt like two frozen lumps of ice and her shabby leather boots did little to keep out the cold as they were too well-worn. She'd never had anything new at all in her short young life. Hand-me-downs from her sister and second-hand goods were the only things that seemed to pass her way.

'Sorry, Pa,' she mumbled as she pulled her hole-ridden woollen shawl around her shoulders in a vain attempt to block out the biting northerly wind. It had been snowing for the past half hour, and when her father had returned home from the pub, drunk as he often was, it had been his idea to go Carol singing again to raise some money— the money he'd already frittered away at The Kings Arms.

'If you didn't keep going out and spending your pitiful wages on drink, we wouldn't need to do this,' Ma grumbled, as she crossed her arms across her chest in an effort to keep warm.

'Bit of fresh air will do the kids the power of good!' he enthused. 'It'll put roses in their cheeks!'

Pa never seemed to feel the cold like the rest of them did.

So far, they'd had three doors slammed firmly shut in their faces and twice they'd wasted time, singing outside a couple of shops until they realised the owners weren't going to come out and pay them a farthing. And no wonder and all, they must have sounded like a cat's chorus. Pa had no musical talent whatsoever as he sang loudly off key, the two little 'uns didn't know the words to the Carols and her elder sister, Eliza, was in a world of her own no doubt thinking about George, her amorous boyfriend, again. It was only she and Ma who had inherited the musical gene. Ma had a sweet voice. Years ago, she'd performed on stage at a local music hall until she met her Bertie. She'd always longed to return, but he'd forbidden such an idea saying she belonged to him now and she wasn't going to flaunt herself on stage in front of a bunch of revellers. Ma had broken her heart after having to give up her music career, but she'd still sang around the home whenever she could and usually it was when Pa was out of the way.

Ma's lips though were now going blue with the cold. She hadn't seemed herself of late and now things she used to do with ease seemed to take a lot longer these days. Angeline helped her mother when she could but Eliza, with her lazy ways, did little to step into the breach preferring to spend time with George Whittle spooning in the alleyway outside their home, which was known as

Christmas Alley. Angeline had no idea why it was called by that name, but she liked it.

One afternoon, when no one else was around, Angeline noticed Ma's breathing was funny, she'd been wheezing and gasping for air. Between breaths, she'd given Angeline instructions to run to the pub a couple of doors away to fetch a nip of brandy in an old tin mug. Angeline had moved at lightning speed and handed over the couple of coins Ma had given her to the big-chested barmaid who worked there.

When she'd returned, bolting up the stairs, two at a time, she'd stood by the bed, her hand trembling as she looked at her poor mother. Bringing the mug to Ma's lips, her mother had slowly drank it and her blue lips became pink again and her breathing seemed to settle down into a normal rhythm. But the tot of brandy to help Ma got to be a habit and now, almost not a day went by when her mother didn't need a nip of something alcoholic. So, while she was yelling at Pa not to spend their money at the taverns in the area, she was doing something similar herself, though on not such a grand scale.

The twinkling Christmas lights from the holly-decorated shops on the High Street cheered Angeline's heart. There was one shop in particular where she loved to peer in the window and that was Mr Sampson's, the grocer's store. She often peered in the shop's bay window when she was out selling boxes of matches to help the family finances. Angeline loved the shop window so much because amongst all the Christmas goodies in the window there: the plum puddings, figs, dates, oranges and apples and even the gift-wrapped boxes of luxury chocolates, was a small wooden nativity set. She'd stand for ages gazing in through the frosted window at that particular scene. The baby Jesus lay in a straw-filled manger, with his beautiful mother, Mary, by his side looking serene and composed, and his father, Joseph, protectively stood behind her. Then there were the shepherds who stood in awe with their cattle and sheep close by and the three Magi who knelt to offer gifts of gold, frankincense and myrrh to the newborn King. Oh, how she loved that scene because Mr Sampson had made a silver star that was suspended above it, just over the baby's manger.

Mr and Mrs Sampson would often smile at her when she passed by selling matches from the wicker basket hooked over the crook of her arm. Her mother had worked at the Bryant and May match factory at Bow, until she became sick, forcing her to leave. Lucky though, she hadn't got that phossy jaw condition many spoke about because Ma had told her that was a very bad thing. It actually killed some folk and even if they didn't die, they ended up in agony from it as their teeth and jaws rotted away. But something had made Ma have lung problems as she often coughed and wheezed, and maybe it was working at that place that might have caused it.

Sometimes, if it was a bitterly cold day, Mrs Sampson would beckon Angeline inside the store and tell her to sit by the fireside in the back room, then she'd fetch her a hot toddy to warm her up. But, regretfully, she couldn't stay there forever as there were matches that needed selling.

When Ma left the factory, she became a home worker instead for a spell, assembling matchboxes with the children in their home until she no longer had the energy to do so and that was the end of that. So to make ends meet, Angeline got herself a job as a street seller. Pa was a chimney sweep but as he didn't seem to work all that often these days, only she and her brother Michael brought any extra money into the home to make up for their father's reluctance to get stuck into a hard day's graft. Michael worked at a local butcher shop and often took out the deliveries on a barrow for them. He was handsome and all, fit and strong as her father had once been, but today he was at work. So many people were purchasing meat and poultry for the festive season that he was rushed off his feet.

'Come along, girl! Don't dawdle!' Pa bellowed. 'We'll stop by here and sing *Oh come all ye faithful*. You did teach the kids the words last night, like I asked you to, Angeline?'

She nodded. It had been hard work trying to get Sammy and Joanna to learn the words and she wasn't entirely sure they knew them all now.

'*Oh come holly faithful...*' Sammy began, which weren't exactly the correct words she'd taught them but it made her smile.

'*Joyful and the trumpet...*'

Angeline began to chuckle and caught her father's piercing gaze. 'This is not a laughing matter!' he glowered. A trickle of fear ran down her spine and not wanting to get on her father's bad side, she said, 'Sorry, Pa. I did teach them the words but they've obviously not understood them.'

He shook his head. 'Let's try another then... come on altogether, *The Holly and the Ivy*...' Making semicircular motions in the air with his index finger as though conducting them all, he then stood beside them and joined in.

This time Angeline didn't laugh, she didn't even smile, but she and her mother sang the song beautifully, harmonising with one another as everyone else stopped singing, allowing them to have their special moment. An elderly, well-dressed couple, passed by and dropped some coins into Pa's metal cup. 'That brought a tear to my eye...' The lady smiled.

'Thank ye kindly!' Pa doffed his battered top hat, the one he'd been given many years ago when he'd swept the chimneys in one of the big houses in the area. Mrs Billington, the house owner, had seemed to like Pa and often gave him little gifts. The hat had been her late husband's and was in pristine condition when it had been given to Pa. Now though, it looked shabby and worn, a bit like her father himself, Angeline supposed.

The gentleman smiled and nodded his head at the group, before taking the lady by the arm and escorting her in the direction of the high street.

'A few more like that we could do with,' Pa said, grinning widely as he displayed a missing tooth and a stubbled chin. Angeline hoped the couple hadn't noticed his beery breath or that he was swaying ever so slightly from side to side.

Within the hour, the snow had got so heavy they had to return home. 'Well, we didn't collect from many,' Pa said with a grin, 'but that couple rewarded us handsomely!'

Rewarded us? It was only me and Ma who sang there! Angeline kept her thoughts to herself.

'At least now I can buy us all some food for Christmas day,' Ma whispered. Then they all trailed behind her as she entered the butcher shop, which had a collapsible wooden placard outside, which read: *M. B. Styles and Sons: purveyors of fine quality meat and Poultry.*

Michael stood behind the long counter with a newspaper-wrapped parcel of meat for them: chicken, sausages and bacon. Suspended from the ceiling just behind him, were several silver hooks bearing pieces of poultry and small joints of meat.

Ma went to pay him, pulling out her purse from her skirt pocket, but the butcher, Mr Styles, shook his head and waved her hand away. 'No need for any payment, Mrs Barker, this is on me!' he said, his chubby whiskered chops breaking into a wide grin.

'Your son works hard for me.'

Ma looked at the man as she teared up. 'Thank you so much, Mr Styles. That is so kind of you.'

Angeline noticed the gleam in her father's eyes, suspecting he had plans for that money Ma had just saved. Narrowing her gaze, she noticed he was red-faced now and propping himself up against the black and white wall tiles, his feet almost sliding through the layer of sawdust scattered on the floor. A sense of mortification washed over Angeline as her father hiccupped loudly. Why on earth did he have to keep shaming them all?

Chapter Two

The Barker home was a set of rented rooms located in a huddle of streets near the match factory at Bow. On the way there, Angeline told her parents she'd be calling to see Mrs Sampson at the shop.

'Perhaps she'll give you something for Christmas. If she offers you anything ask for a box of chocolates!' her father chuckled, ever the one for getting something out of others. 'I know she 'as a special liking for you as she's always calling you inside that shop out of the cold. You should exploit the situation more!' He grinned.

Disgusted, Angeline carried on trudging through the snow-covered pavement, she couldn't wait to get in from the cold and sit in front of the fire. There'd be no fire back at their house, it hadn't even been lit that day and earlier she'd sat shivering, warming her hands on the light of a short stubby candle.

'That's not why I'm going there,' she whispered behind the palm of her hand to her mother as they walked behind Pa, with Eliza and the two little ones trailing behind.

'I know that, ducks. Don't take any notice of 'im,' Ma said, squeezing her daughter's hand in reassurance.

Leaving her family on the corner for them to turn into Christmas Alley, Angeline glanced towards the shop to see with delight that now there was a large candle added to the advent display, which flickered and added a warm glow to the nativity scene.

Spotting Angeline at the window as the snowflakes continued to fall settling on her hair and nose, Mrs Sampson beckoned her to step inside.

Angeline smiled broadly as she stepped through the door as the woman opened it for her. A little bell tinkled on entering, it alerted the Sampsons that a customer had arrived. Angeline gasped as she saw just how Christmassy the shop now looked with garlands of holly and ivy strung from the eaves and with flickering coloured lanterns, here and there, it brought a glow to her heart. And near the wooden counter in the corner was a beautiful fir tree, trimmed and decked with miniature candles which were now alight.

She swallowed a lump in her throat, the whole scene was bringing tears to her eyes.

'Take your shawl and boots off, child,' Mrs Sampson said firmly. 'I'll fetch you a nice warm blanket and you can toast those toes by the fire in the back room with me. Mr Sampson can manage on his own for a while. Even though it's Christmas Eve, we're quiet at the moment as there aren't many venturing out in this snowstorm.'

Angeline nodded and smiled. Then Mrs Sampson led her through to the backroom, taking her shawl and putting it to dry out, stretching it over a wooden clothes horse which she propped up near the fire, and the boots she put in the fireplace itself to dry out.

'Now then, when we've had some hot chocolate and a nice plate of my special mince pies and a good old chin wag, Mr Sampson will walk you back home.'

'Oh, I couldn't expect him to do that for me!' Angeline's eyes grew large. 'He's a busy man.'

'Nonsense, dear. I should never forgive myself if I allowed you to walk home alone in this snowstorm.'

Angeline knew it was no use arguing, so she took an armchair by the fire to sit in whilst Mrs Sampson draped a thick woollen blanket over her. Watching the flames of the fire dance around in the grate, and listening to the comfortable crackle, she thought she'd never felt so cosy in all her life.

Entering with a tray containing the cups of chocolate and a plate of mince pies, Mrs Sampson set it down on a small occasional table between the two armchairs. She handed a cup to Angeline and took one for herself. 'Now what brings you out and about on such a day as this?' she asked.

'Pa took us out Carol singing...' she said, then she took a sip of the thick sweet drink that was so velvety smooth, she was in heaven as it warmed her to the core.

Mrs Sampson quirked a brow. 'In this weather?'

Angeline inclined her head. How could she explain what her father was like? A disappointment to them all. She felt she ought to make some sort of excuse for him. 'We weren't out all that long...'

Mrs Sampson nodded. 'I suppose this snow did arrive rather quickly this afternoon. It's caught us all out.'

After they'd eaten and finished their hot chocolate, Angeline noticed that Mrs Sampson's eyes were glittering, almost as though she had some sort of secret or surprise. 'Just you stay there,' she said, 'I've got a Christmas present for you.'

Mrs Sampson left the room, returning a short while later cradling a dark blue box in her arms that was tied with a light blue satin ribbon. She was carrying it as if it were a newborn babe. At first, Angeline thought it was a shoe box, the woman had commented that she needed a new pair of leather boots just the other day. But then as Mrs Sampson handed it to her, the woman stepped back and smiled.

'Just be careful how you open it as it's quite delicate,' she enthused.

Not a new pair of boots, then?

Angeline's heartbeat quickened as she laid the box on the table and unwrapped the bow, removing the lid. The inside of the box was covered in a layer of white tissue paper. Gently, she drew back the paper, her breath catching in her throat. Gazing down in awe, she gasped. It was the most beautiful porcelain doll she'd ever seen in her life, dressed in a white satin gown, sparkling with diamantes. The doll's face had bright blue eyes and a cascade of blonde hair. It was then she noticed the wings.

'It's an angel,' said Mrs Sampson softly. 'As soon as I saw her, I thought of your name as you're Angeline and we often shorten it to Angel.'

Angeline's eyes began to fill with tears, she couldn't believe someone could be capable of such kindness. She'd never owned a real doll bought from a proper shop in all her life, the only doll she'd ever owned was Rosie and she'd been made out of rags by her mother, but she'd loved that doll to death until it had fallen apart at the seams.

'Oh, thank you so much, Mrs Sampson,' she said, wiping her tears away with the back of her hand.

The woman dipped into her pinafore pocket to hand her a handkerchief. 'There, there, child. Wipe your eyes, I didn't think giving you a present would cause you to cry.' She clicked her tongue and shook her head. 'I hope I haven't upset you?'

'You haven't. They are tears of happiness,' Angeline sniffed, setting herself off again.

Hearing a tinkle from the shop bell, Mrs Sampson said, 'I'll leave you to compose yourself and go to see how my husband's doing in the shop, I won't be a tick, dear, ' she said and she winked at Angeline.

When the woman had departed, she sat ̩
at the doll, taking the time to enjoy the bea
gift. She'd never seen anything as beautiful
her born days.

Mrs Sampson returned later, a frown pucke
her forehead. 'The snow's coming down thick
fast, so I've told Mr Sampson he'd better walk
home right now,' she said. 'We're going to shut
shop for the rest of the day. Put your boots on a
fetch your shawl from the clothes horse.'

In some ways, Angeline thought she mig
spend a happier Christmas if she were trapped i
the shop with the Sampsons, but then she fe
guilty for thinking that way as Ma and the kid
needed her.

When she was ready to leave, Angeline hugged
the woman, who loaned her a pair of her woollen
gloves and a scarf to wear on her way home.
'Mr Sampson will bring them back with him,'
she explained when Angeline had protested she
couldn't possibly take them from her.

Something that concerned Angeline though
was how her sister would react when she
discovered that she'd been given such a beautiful
gift. Would she be jealous of her good fortune?
They were both too old to play with dolls, of
course, this one was more of a decorative doll. She
could well imagine it adorning some rich young
girl's dressing table, something to be admired and
enjoyed.

**

Mr Sampson left Angeline at the scuffed back door of her home. She hated anyone coming near the house as she often wondered what they must think of its shabby state. She handed him the gloves and scarf and thanked him for the gift. Smiling warmly, he said, 'Merry Christmas, Angel. The shop will be shut for a couple of days over the festive season, but we hope we see you soon over the Christmas period...'

'Merry Christmas, Mr Sampson,' she smiled, as carefully she held on to the gift box and made her way to the door. What a contrast it was though when she pushed it open. The room was dark and icy cold. Why had no one even lit a fire yet? The grate was just filled with old coke and ashes. She placed the box on the table beneath the window and taking a match from its box, she struck a light and lit both the half-used candle on the windowsill and the one on the mantelpiece.

The house seemed deathly quiet. Where was everyone?

'Ma?' she shouted. No reply. So she called again.

Then she heard it, the sobbing. It sounded like one of the kids, she rushed up the stairs to her bedroom to find Sammy and Joanna huddled together on her bed crying their eyes out.

'What's wrong?' she asked.

Joanna gazed up at her with big china-blue eyes, moist with tears as she draped her arm around Sammy's shoulders. Taking a huge shuddering sob before saying, 'He...he's gone, Angel.'

'Who's gone, darlin'?'

'Pa,' Sammy said, wiping his nose on the back of his jacket sleeve.

'Gone? You mean to the pub?'

'No, he's gone off with that bleedin' floozie!' Angeline turned to see Eliza standing behind her. 'Good riddance I say an' all.'

'You mean he's never coming back?'

'No, not by all accounts!' Eliza folded her arms and thrust out her chin in a determined fashion.

'What's a floozie?' Sammy sniffed.

'Never you flamin' mind,' said Eliza, then she ushered Angeline out of the room and once behind the door, whispered. 'You know the sort I mean, don't you? Her at The Kings Arms!'

Angeline's mouth popped open. She did know her indeed as she was the big-busted barmaid who had served her many a time with a tot of brandy for Ma. But why would Pa be going off with her?

Eliza placed her hands on both hips and tossed back her red hair. 'Ma should have seen this coming,' she said angrily as her brown eyes flashed furiously.

Angeline frowned. 'Where is she right now?'

'She's gone to see if she can pawn something to Mr Goodman.'

'Surely not her wedding ring again?'

'No, that went a long time ago to pay off Pa's debts.'

Angeline frowned. Come to think of it, she'd not seen Ma wear her wedding ring for a long time.

'What then?'

'Remember that pretty pearl brooch Granny Ivy gave her?'

Angeline nodded. She did remember it indeed. 'She can't do that, I won't allow her to!' she said stamping her foot. 'I have something she can pawn instead.'

Eliza's eyes widened. 'How can you have anything worth pawning, Angeline? You get all your cast-offs from me!'

'Mrs Sampson gave me a Christmas present today, it might be worth something, it's in the living room on the table.'

Eliza pushed past her sister, almost knocking her against the wall, running quickly down the stairs until she reached the table, where, without even asking, she hurriedly unwrapped the gift.

'Be careful with it, it's easily broken,' Angeline pleaded.

Eliza's eyes widened and her breath became short and sharp as she gazed in awe at the angel inside. 'How come no one ever gives me anything like this?' she complained. 'Whatcha done to deserve it?' She thrust out her bottom lip as she often did when she had a fit of pouting.

Angeline shrugged. 'Don't know, but it's nice, isn't it?'

'Yes, it's lovely,' Eliza said, enchanted by the beautiful angel, her eyes softening now.

'If I weren't going to pawn it, I'd share it with you, Eliza. We'd take turns, but I reckon we need the money more than we need the angel!'

Eliza nodded. Even she could see the sense of what her sister was saying.

Suddenly, the front door flew open and Ma entered, bringing a flurry of snowflakes and a cold blast of air in with her. Her cheeks looked pinched and red from the cold but her lips were blue. Her once fit-looking body, now seemed hunched over like the elderly woman Angeline knew who sold flowers in the square. Their ma wasn't that old either, she was probably half that woman's age but now her whole demeanour seemed to spell defeat.

'Come and sit down, Ma,' Angeline said, her voice full of concern as she guided her mother towards a chair near the table.

It was then Eliza seemed to break out of her reverie and realise what was going on. 'Yes, Ma, sit down. Remove your shawl, I'll fetch a blanket from your bed and Angel can make you a cup of tea.'

Their mother nodded and then coughed harshly into her fisted hand. When she recovered, she patted Eliza's shoulder before saying, 'Yer girls are so good to me.'

'Did you manage to get anything for the brooch, Ma?' Eliza asked in expectation.

Ma shook her head sadly. 'The shop was shut by the time I got there. I don't know what we're going to do, girls—we've got no money left at all now. Yer father's done a runner with that tarty one from the pub, taken all we had left including that bit of money we just made from the singing. All I got in the house for Christmas is a bit o' bread and scrape and a pan of leftover pearl barley soup.'

'But what about that parcel of meat the butcher gave us?' Angeline blinked.

Eliza fiercely shook her head, her vibrant locks bouncing on her shoulders. 'He took that with him when he left here. Probably wants to sell it in the pub!'

Angeline could hardly believe her ears that their father would steal from his own flesh and blood like that. He'd done some rotten things in his time but this took the flamin' biscuit!

'If the pawn shop's not open, I'm taking that angel to see if I can sell it somewhere. We've got to eat.'

'What angel?'

Her mother furrowed her brow and coughed again.

'The Sampsons bought me a beautiful angel doll, Ma. It's in that box over there on the windowsill.'

Ma lifted her head to look. She didn't even have enough strength to pull herself up from the chair right now. 'You stay where you are, Ma. I'll bring it to you,' Angeline said.

Her mother's eyes brightened when Angeline opened the box and drew back the tissue paper to reveal the decorative doll inside.

'That's so beautiful,' their mother gasped putting a palm to her chest, 'but I can't allow you to sell it, it was a gift.'

'Nonsense,' said Eliza, 'Angeline can see the

sense in us all having something to eat over Christmas and we need coal for the fire, this place is like the North Pole.' She shivered involuntary.

Ma nodded. 'I know you girls are both right, but I feel so guilty that we all 'ave to suffer like this, particularly over Christmas. This is the hardest winter I've known since I was a child.'

Angeline replaced the doll in the box and went to make them all a cup of tea, realising they'd have to reuse the same tea leaves as there was no money left to buy any more. Eliza went off to fetch Ma a blanket.

As Angeline brewed the tea, she peered out of the scullery window to see some people trudging through the snow, the sound of laughter drifting towards her. A group of children were pelting snowballs at one another. How she wished she could be one of those children enjoying the snow but her boots had holes in them and her shawl would barely offer her protection against the weather. What kind of a Christmas could they all expect now?

***

'C'mon, hurry up, will you?' Eliza shouted as Angeline trailed behind her, the cold wind hitting the back of her throat, making her gasp for breath.

Eliza paused for a moment. 'Here, let me carry the box,' she said crossly. But Angeline just shook her head, at least for the time being it was still all hers, even though she realised soon it might belong to another.

'We'll try here in this shop,' Eliza pointed to the toy shop which still appeared to be open as there was a light on inside, even though the street was all but deserted apart from the two girls.

Angeline gazed at the colourful carousel in the middle of the window display, the white horses were at varying heights. It was musical too, she knew because she'd gone in there once with Michael and they'd asked the shopkeeper permission to wind it up so they might watch the horses bob up and down and they'd listened to the tinkling music. Besides that, on the right, was a large china doll with bright eyes and long lustrous eyelashes, and to the left, a blue wooden sailing boat complete with white sails and multicoloured flags.

The shop was packed to the rafters with all manner of toys: spinning tops, doll's houses, wooden trains, hoops and balls and lots of other things. Apart from the Sampson's store, it was her favourite.

Eliza made to walk inside but the door was jammed shut. 'Damn and blast!' she said, stamping her foot.

'Try knocking instead,' Angeline urged, 'I can see there's a light in the back room.'

Eliza knocked and when she got no reply, she knocked harder, bringing the elderly shopkeeper to the door. He unlocked it, screwing up his face in annoyance. 'We're closed!' he barked, as he looked them up and down as though they were a curiosity to him.

'We don't want to buy nothin', sir,' Angeline sniffed, 'we wanna sell something to you.'

The man narrowed his eyes. ''Ere, I don't sell no stolen goods...'

'What we have ain't stolen,' Eliza explained. 'Me sister was given a beautiful gift today but we'd rather have the money instead with things being tight over Christmas and all.'

'I see,' he said, with a thoughtful look in his grey eyes. 'You'd better step inside...'

As both girls embraced the warmth of the shop, Angeline wondered how they'd convince the man he'd like to buy the angel.

Chapter Three

'Hmmm, quite good quality,' the shopkeeper said, turning the doll over on the counter and lifting its lace-edged dress to examine it in closer detail. 'Made in France.'

'How do you know that?' Eliza asked.

The man tapped the side of his nose with his index finger, and then he chuckled. 'It says so on the back of the doll. How did you come by it?'

'Mr and Mrs Sampson gave it to me as a gift today,' Angeline said, with more than a tone of regret in her voice. 'I don't want to get rid of it as it's the loveliest thing I've ever owned in my life.'

The man smiled. 'But I guess your family needs the money?' He asked studying them over the top of his round silver spectacles.

She nodded.

'Aren't you two Bertie Barker's kids?'

'Yes, we are!' Eliza said crossly. 'And he's gorn and left us all on Christmas Eve an' all.'

'Poor kids,' the man muttered beneath his breath. 'Look, I'll tell you what I can do instead of immediately selling it. I could raffle it for you.'

Eliza glared at him, her eyes hooded with suspicion. 'Raffle it? I don't know what that is.'

'A raffle takes place when numbered tickets are sold for a special prize or prizes,' the shopkeeper explained. 'Now, if you get my meaning, if I raffled this here angel doll for say a penny a ticket, many folk might be able to afford that. Then after a week or so, I could do what they call a draw. That means someone picking out the winning ticket from a hat or a box, something like that. The winner gets the prize and we might make more money that way too.'

Eliza's eyes lit up. 'I like the sound of that,' she said brightly, clasping her hands together.

'You could even buy a ticket yourselves, girls,' the shopkeeper suggested.

Angeline shook her head vigorously. 'We haven't got a farthing never mind a penny, mister.'

'Then I shall give you a penny as a gift from me and you can purchase a ticket. That way you'll have the chance to win your doll back and make some money in the process!'

'Me sister and me shall 'ave to discuss this,' Eliza said as if she was an adult and not a fifteen-year-old.

'Very well,' the shopkeeper nodded, 'I'll just be out the back room for a moment.'

'We can't do this,' Eliza hissed when he'd left the room.

'Why not?' Angeline wanted to know.

'Because for all we know he might be swindling us. A penny indeed! He's buying the doll for a penny!'

'I see what you mean, but it might be our only offer.'

'Yes, and if we go along with what he has in mind, we don't even get to see the penny as it goes towards a ticket for the doll. I think we better say no.'

Crestfallen, Angeline nodded in agreement.

They left the shop dispirited, it was obvious the shopkeeper wanted to make money out of them.

'What now?' Angeline said, shoving her hands deep into her dress pockets. If only they'd even had a pair of gloves to share between them.

'What about if we go back home for now and wait until Mr Goodman opens up his pawn shop? You never know he might open it in the morning?' Eliza said hopefully.

'I doubt it, it's Christmas day tomorrow!' Angeline puffed out a breath of steam wishing she still had Mrs Sampson's warm woollen gloves on her hands.

'You're forgetting something,' Eliza's eyes gleamed. 'Mr Goodman doesn't celebrate Christmas! He's a different religion to us. So, he might well open his shop!'

There was still hope. If they could manage overnight and go to the shop first thing in the morning then maybe Christmas in the Barker home would not be cancelled after all.

***

'He's done what?' Michael blinked in horror. 'Are my ears deceiving me?' He had just finished work for the day, having taken out several deliveries on the wooden hand cart for Mr Styles. This was just all too much.

Ma raised her head from where she'd been staring down into her teacup at the leaves remaining at the bottom of the cup for the past few minutes while Angeline and Eliza had been out in the snow.

'Your father has left us and taken all the money we had from my purse, along with that parcel of meat your employer gave us for Christmas, Michael.'

Michael put his head in his hands for a moment, then dropped them to his sides as he looked at his mother. 'What a terrible thing to do to us all. Mr Styles went out of his way to give us that meat with his kind generosity, and in a way I bleedin' earned it an' all. I've been working every moment God sends there, we've been so busy my legs have ached and my back feels like it's been cut in 'alf and all for the sake of that rotten no-good father of mine to take everything with him. Where's he gone to? I've a good mind to rush there now and punch his bleedin' lights out!' He curled his hands into fists at his side.

Ma had never seen him look so angry before. He was growing up that was for sure. Becoming a man who was as tall as his own father.

'He's gone off with that floozie one from the pub, her what used to serve you all that nip o' brandy for me ailment...' Ma said sadly.

Michael drew up close to his mother and draped a comforting arm around her shoulder. Then he leant over to softly peck her cheek. 'I don't like to see you so upset like this Ma, but that man is no longer welcome here after the way he's treated you over the years. I could go around and give him what for but I doubt it would do any good, so instead I'm going to run back to the butcher shop as Mr Styles will be there for a while yet. I won't tell him what's happened though, I'll ask him if I can buy some meat out of my next lot of earnings as a special Christmas treat for us. Maybe he'll let me 'ave some leftover offcuts as well—they won't be the best but we can boil them up for soup, should see us through the festive season and he did have a few sausages left too.'

Ma patted her son's hand. 'You're a good boy, if yer see yer sisters out there, tell them to hurry home afore it gets dark!' she warned.

He nodded, then turning on his heel, he made to go through the front door and as a gust of wind blew cold frosted air into the room, he turned to blow his mother a kiss, giving her some hope for the future.

Without Bertie around, she realised they would be far better off, all of them, even now if her side of the bed was empty. She could offer to share it now with one of the girls to keep warm as they were all cramped in the other bedroom. Yes, that's what they'd do from now on. All the girls would be in one bedroom and the boys in another.

Realising Sammy and Joanna had gone quiet as she'd been revelling in her despair, she went to fetch them finding them both lying on the girls' bed huddled together.

'Come on, kids,' she shouted, trying to sound full of life, 'come into the living room with me, Christmas is about to begin!'

***

Ma and the kids had decorated the living room with some decorations cut from old newspaper and they strung paper stars and snowflakes around the room and hung a branch of holly with red berries over the mantelpiece, and there was now a fire kindling in the grate.

'Now, we're just waiting for Angeline and Eliza,' Ma said with a look of concern on her face. Darkness had already descended, and in her mind, Ma envisioned the pair of them huddled in a corner somewhere, unable to get home due to the heavy snowfall.

'Shall I go and look for them?' Michael asked. He'd returned with a package of scrag end lamb which would do for a stew, a few sausages and some bones for boiling. If Mr Styles was puzzled, he hadn't said so. But maybe he's already guessed his father was a wrong 'un.

Ma nodded. 'If you would, Michael, there's a good lad. Give it another ten minutes before you venture out there, you need a bit of a rest after the day you've had.' After experiencing such a trying afternoon, all Ma wanted was all her kids with her under one roof, safe, sound and at least warm and fed for the time being. Who knew though how long the supplies would hold out for?

***

Eliza and Angeline trudged through the ankle-deep snow in Christmas Alley. Since leaving the house, their tracks had been covered by a fresh fall of snow. The only light to illuminate their path was from a nearby gaslight at the alley's entrance. Angeline was keen to get inside the house but Eliza seemed to be taking her time.

I bet it's because she wants to see George, Angeline thought. *But even he would be a fool to come out in this weather.*

'Here, give me that!' Eliza grabbed the angel doll in its box from Angeline's grasp.

'Hey!' she protested. 'Give that back to me right now!'

'Well, you did say we could share it!' Her sister retorted.

That was true but Angeline hadn't imagined sharing her doll in the alleyway.

Quick as a flash, her sister removed the doll from its box and was holding it up over her head. Angeline grabbed the box before it got damp from the snow.

'Oh Angel, oh Angel, beautiful Angel!' Eliza said in a mocking tone of voice.

'What do you think you're doing?'

Angeline made to grab for the doll but Eliza whisked it away in a taunting fashion.

'Angel, come to save us!' She said, squealing with laughter.

Before Angeline had a chance to say anything she watched as her sister trembled from top to toe, her mouth agape.

There, in front of them both was a ball of golden light. It radiated both warmth and peace.

'What's going on?' Angeline asked.

'I've no idea.' Her sister seemed mesmerised by the sight before them.

Angeline grabbed the angel doll from Eliza's grasp and started to rush towards home. Whatever they'd just seen she didn't understand, but at least it had stopped her sister from taunting her.

The thick snow was now well above her ankles. She didn't turn to look behind her until she arrived at the door and by then the ball of light was becoming smaller and smaller until it eventually disappeared from view, and Eliza rushed to catch up with her sister, bundling up her skirts to move faster.

'What happened there?' Eliza asked breathlessly. 'Did we really see that light?'

'I don't know but we're both cold and hungry. Perhaps we imagined the whole thing or maybe it was the sun trying to shine through the clouds!'

Angeline shook her head, it was too late for the sun as now it was almost dark. Sincerely doubting the whole event they'd just witnessed, she thrust open the door and stepped inside the threshold of their house, gasping as she saw the paper decorations suspended from the ceiling, and a fire burning in the grate.

Eliza stumbled in behind her and closing the door, asked with a big smile on her face, 'Where did you get the coal from, Ma?'

'Our Michael collected it from the coal merchant's yard before he closed for Christmas, he was just going to go out to look for you pair, I was getting a bit concerned where you were.'

'Sorry, Ma,' Angeline smiled at their mother, not wishing for all the world to worry her right now.

Ma nodded. 'The merchant only had a small bucketful to sell him though, and to be truthful, that's all Michael could afford anyhow. He's had a sub from the butcher and also asked him if he could have some scrag ends for stew and some sausages as well as bones for boiling. And we've even got a sack of spuds!' she said proudly. 'So maybe we can have some sort of Christmas after all!'

***

When Angeline lay cuddled up in bed beside Eliza that night with the two young 'uns sleeping softly on pallets on the floor, she gazed up at the frosty star-speckled sky, it had now ceased snowing and she wondered what Christmas day held in store for them all.

Chapter Four

On Christmas morning, Angeline awoke early and drew back the curtains to peer through the frosted windowpane. The slate grey sky told her there was more snow on the way. She surveyed the heavy fall they'd had since yesterday and observed the quietness outside the window. There were no sounds of costermonger carts, no babble of excited voices—complete silence, except for thick sections of snow sliding off the roof.

She watched and smiled as Eliza still slept in the bed they both shared, letting out the occasional gentle snore here and there. Their younger brother and sister were still fast asleep on their straw-filled pallets.

After all, what was the point in them waking up early when for them Christmas day would be like any other? There'd be no gifts for anyone to enjoy this year, no full bellies stuffed to the hilt with a roast goose dinner and plum pudding, no happy smiles. How could Pa have sold all that meat and poultry from the butcher's to ne'er do wells at the pub?

Ma stood in the doorway and beckoned Angeline to her side with her index finger. 'I'm sorry, love,' she said with a heavy sigh. 'It's not the Christmas we were expecting...'

Angeline wrapped her arms around her mother's waist and hugged her. 'We'll manage somehow, Ma,' she comforted.

Her mother's face creased into a frown. 'But what if we can't get out? What if we get holed up for days on end? There's no let up to this snow.'

'Don't worry, Ma, if push comes to shove our Michael will dig us out of here, and Mr and Mrs Sampson won't see us starve, either. They're not too far away.'

Ma raised an angry fist. 'Sorry, but I could bleedin' kill that father of yours!'

Truth be told, Angeline felt she could kill Pa herself for leaving them all in the lurch like this. But deep down, she wondered if Ma was worried because she wouldn't be able to have her daily tot of brandy. If they couldn't get out, would that mean she'd suffer? It did seem to help but Angeline worried in case she was getting too reliant on it and it now cost money they didn't have. Ma's cough had become racking of late and left her all but worn out. Her skeletal figure and her prominent cheekbones made her brown eyes look huge and hollow and her skin seemed to have a yellowy tinge of late. This wasn't the mother she'd always known, this mother looked like a shadow of her former self.

Angeline followed her mother downstairs and they both helped to light the fire, realising they now had to be careful in case they ran out of fuel. There were only a few lumps of coal left in the coal scuttle.

'We'll get this going, Ma,' Angeline said cheerfully, 'that'll make us feel better.'

'But we'll have to go sparingly with the firewood and coal though,' her mother warned. 'That bucketful Michael managed to fetch won't last forever.'

Angeline nodded. 'At least we can be warm on Christmas day and cook some food on the fire, even if it wasn't the feast we'd imagined. Some ain't so lucky.'

She thought of the beggars of all ages she saw on the streets of the Old Nichol—which was a hodgepodge of courts and streets where the housing and sanitation were poor. Its inhabitants would do anything for a crust of bread, there were even mothers with babes in arms, begging on the street. What chance did they stand?

'Maybe the snow will stop falling by tomorrow and I can get outside to sell some more matches.'

Her mother nodded and smiled, but it did not quite reach her eyes—she could see the fear there behind it all.

How on earth had they got themselves into this position? Pa had a lot to answer for.

Tears filled Angeline's eyes and she wiped them away with the back of her hand before her mother could notice her distress. There was no use in upsetting Ma, it would only set her back in her condition but it just didn't seem fair to have been given such a lovely present of that angel doll when the rest of the family had to go without.

Of course, Mr and Mrs Sampson would have absolutely no idea of how things were for her at home. Ma never shopped at that place as she hardly ever went outside the door these days, such was her poor health. Pa only shopped at places where he felt he would get a bargain, they sold things off cheap or maybe they'd bought knock-off gear to sell. The Sampsons hadn't a clue.

Within half an hour, the fire was flickering in the grate and Angeline warmed her blue fingers before it. At least they'd have some food and warmth, even if it only lasted for a day.

***

'I'll lay the table, Ma,' Angeline offered later that day as a delicious aroma arose from the hearth where Ma was boiling a pan of lamb stew.

Her mother let out a little laugh. 'Lay the table with the best cloth, we might as well.'

Angeline raised her eyebrows. Ma never used that fine white linen cloth, she reckoned she was keeping it for best, but unfortunately there never seemed to be a time when it was best to use it.

'Why now, Ma?' She asked.

Her mother secured the pan on the fire, then she stood and turned towards her daughter. 'Why not now?' she said with hands on hips. 'Today's Christmas day, ain't it?' Angeline nodded, but frowned, as if she was missing the point of it all.

'Don't look at me daft, child!' Ma said, throwing her hands in mid-air. 'Don't you see? That fine Irish linen tablecloth was a wedding present to me and your father and I've only ever got to use it a handful of times. Now he's gorn, I might as well make use of it. What's the point in keeping it for best? In any case, today is a special day even if we ain't got no fine food or presents, we can make the most of it.'

Angeline smiled ruefully, then went off to the sideboard drawer where she pulled out the cloth which was embroidered in all sorts of colours with pretty flowers and green ivy, it was ever so pretty and just using it cheered her heart. She had an idea. 'How about I put out those nice china cups you never use too, Ma?'

'Aye, that's a good idea!' There was a spark in her mother's eyes now. 'They were another wedding present. Those were from Granny Ivy, bought them in Petticoat Lane, she did. One's a bit chipped but they're ever so pretty and will go with the cloth. You make us all a pot of tea, but don't throw the leaves away, we'll have to reuse them.'

Angeline nodded. Of course they would, sometimes they reused them so much that it seemed as though there was just hot water and a spot of milk in their cups. Those times the tea didn't taste of much either. Angeline longed to taste a cup of coffee, she loved the aroma as the Sampsons sometimes drank it. Many coffee taverns were springing up around the place—she'd been told they were to encourage people to keep away from the evils of drink. It was a pity her Pa didn't take to coffee instead of the ale. Briefly, she wondered what he was doing right now. Was his fancy woman making him a Christmas dinner? She guessed not. Didn't look like there was much at all domesticated about that one.

When Angeline had finished laying the table and had placed a sprig of holly complete with red berries in the middle of it as a centrepiece, she sighed. It did look nice and all. They couldn't afford a Christmas tree, it was the same every year, though last year Pa had dragged one home from the pub with him claiming he'd bought it off some fella or another, but was it a coincidence that some had got stolen from outside one of the shops on the high street around the same time?

'Go and call the kids!' Ma ordered. 'So we can all eat at the same time while it's hot.'

Then Ma went to fetch the pot of lamb stew. It did smell good with onions, carrots and potatoes. It would go far and maybe last a couple of days. Her mother would probably add some dumplings to it when it was running low to eke it out even further.

Angeline's stomach growled with hunger as her mouth moistened in anticipation of what was to come. Ma laid the pot of stew down in the centre of the table, then she ladled it out into the six awaiting bowls. What was most evident of all though, was Pa's empty chair. Although he hadn't been much of a father or husband to her mother,

Angeline felt a sadness all the same.

During the meal, not much was spoken and the children looked at one another awkwardly from time to time as if trying to comprehend the situation they now found themselves in.

They didn't have a Christmas pudding but Ma had baked some mince pies the day before, so they all had one of those each, which they savoured with relish.

Afterwards, when they were all nicely sated, Angeline cleared the table, Eliza had been asked by Ma to do it but she'd suddenly gone off upstairs leaving Angeline to help. And she knew why and all, she would be peering out of the window to see if she could spot George outside in the alley. She was obviously missing him something rotten. He had a tendency to hang around waiting for her sister to put in an appearance.

There'd been no goose or Christmas pudding this year, but they all had full bellies and were better off than many, particularly those living at the Old Nichol.

They enjoyed their Christmas dinner. For the time being it was all they could afford and Ma said she'd boil the lamb bone up later to make some tasty soup with some extra onions Michael had found on the ground at the marketplace. No doubt having fallen from the display and rolled beneath the stall. He was quick not to get noticed and though technically a theft of sorts, stall holders probably had to accept that the merchandise was soiled and bruised and less likely to make a fuss than if someone nicked something directly from their stall.

It wasn't the Christmas they'd envisaged by any means but at least they were all together as a family with the errant one missing. It was Pa who might be having a lonely old time of it and it served him right and all, Angeline thought.

Eliza though, wasn't so sure. 'I reckon he's still with that tarty one from the pub,' she whispered to Angeline when they were both tucked up in bed that night. Sammy and Joanna were both sound asleep having had a long day of it. As it was Christmas day, both had been allowed to stay up until much later than their usual bedtime and merriment had ensued for a while as they'd played party games like "Blindman's Buff" and "Pass the Parcel" – even though the parcel was just a scarf Ma had knitted which had been wrapped in several sheets of newspaper. Then they'd sang songs with Sammy standing on an old wooden crate intended for firewood. He'd perched on it majestically in front of the hearth as he sang his little heart out. His favourite Carol was "We're Three Kings". Angeline had noticed their mother dab away at her tears with a handkerchief when she thought no one was paying attention, but Angeline had been observant. Was Ma thinking back to Christmases past when she'd been happy with their father? They were all putting on a brave front but it was hard for all of them.

Angeline didn't like to think that their father was with that woman but she'd witnessed firsthand the way she'd been flirting with Pa, leaning against the bar provocatively as she'd whispered in his ear. And he, going red in the fizzog as she did so. Oh, it must have been so flattering for him to have all that attention bestowed on him by the buxom young beauty.

Angeline had been sent out to get a tot of brandy for her mother one time when she felt too ill to go and get it herself and she'd caught the pair at it. Of course, as soon as they'd spied her, they'd broken away from one another. The barmaid had returned to serving at the bar and her father had grinned sheepishly in Angeline's direction and tried making small talk with her. But she was no fool, and although Pa realised his wife was drinking far more than was good for her, he did nothing about it. And that was because it ruddy well suited him! Because if Ma were being sedated with her tots of brandy then she wasn't out looking for him and putting pay to his shenanigans. But then again, that was maybe why Ma drank in the first place because she was well aware he no longer desired her but someone much younger instead who didn't have five kids to care for.

Although it wasn't the Christmas they all planned, it was the Christmas they'd been given that year. For Angeline though, although it was tinged with sadness, she was with the people who meant most to her in all the world.

***

The following morning, the family was awoken by a heavy pounding at the door as though someone were using both fists. Angeline's heart hammered incessantly. No, it couldn't be, could it?

'Mavis, let me in!'

It was Pa stood there, his face blue with the cold as he swayed back and forth and appeared to hiccup. 'Mavis! I'm back home!' he shouted, spotting Angeline at the window. He smiled and called out, 'Lemme in, darlin'!'

Before she had a chance to react, she heard her mother's footsteps behind her and hoped she had the strength to remain firm and not cave into his demands.

Ma struggled to lift the sash window for a moment, but then Michael arrived on the scene and looking at his mother said, "Ere Ma, allow me, I'm head of this house now!'

Their mother nodded her approval and Michael flicked the catch and slowly raised the frosted pane window.

Ma moved to the open window, arms folded as the kids looked at her in expectation. How would she deal with their father?

'Mavis, me love,' Pa said in a sing-song kind of way, almost as though he were serenading her outside.

'Don't yer Mavis me love, me!' she shouted back at him.

'Give us another chance, I know you want to as

you love me and it is the Christmas season an' all…'

'Bertie, I have got a little present for you as it 'appens,' said Ma with a crafty smile on her face. She disappeared for a moment, leaving her husband looking befuddled outside.

The children exchanged confused glances with one another, what could it be? Michael began to chuckle as Ma lifted the chamber pot from beneath the girls' bed.

Pa, who had turned away to glance at an attractive pair of young ladies as they passed by in the alley, turned towards the open window as Ma hid the chamber pot behind her back.

'What is it, me love?' he asked, eyes shining.

'Come closer and I'll show you…' She now held out the pot as she edged nearer the window. As Bertie saw what was aimed at him, he seemed rooted to the spot for a moment while he realised what was about to occur and he made to run for it, but the urine in the pot flowed freely as Ma threw it with some force and it landed over him, soaking him to the skin as steam arose from both his body and his ears.

'Merry Christmas, Bertie, me love!' She greeted and smiled as the kids giggled at the spectacle before them.

Michael draped a protective arm around their mother's shoulder. 'I'm so proud of you, Ma,' he said, 'that's been a long time coming!'.

Chapter Five

'No, whatever you do,' said Ma the following day to Angeline, 'you mustn't part with that doll, dear. Mrs Sampson gave it to you as a special gift because she thinks so highly of you. We'll find a way to manage without the money it might bring. At least we won't starve at any rate with Michael working at the butcher shop. Though I could ruddy well flatten that father of yours with this!' She raised a clenched fist. 'I bet his trollop isn't feeding him up at her place, oh no! That made-up little madam doesn't look as though she could as much as boil a bleedin' egg!'

Angeline supposed it must be hard on her mother knowing her husband had overthrown her for a much younger woman and at Christmas of all times. Of course, this had been brewing for some time, but Ma had buried her head in her many duties as a wife and mother and had probably hoped the fire would burn itself out soon, but obviously, it hadn't.

The best course of action would be to keep going, Angeline thought. With or without Pa they'd survive somehow and today she was going to pawn the angel doll and then she was going back on the streets to sell her matches.

***

Mr Goodman, the pawnbroker, offered Angeline two shillings and sixpence for the doll. She'd been hoping for more—enough at least to pay the rent, but reluctantly, she accepted it. The rooms cost three shillings a week, they could make up the remainder with the money they got for her matches. At least if she cobbled enough money together for the rent, Michael would have enough from his wages to pay for food and some fuel for the fire. But what if Ma asked for her tot of brandy? So far, she hadn't and Angeline guessed it must be difficult for her to resist.

Pocketing the money into a little leather purse on a string, she placed it over her head and hid it inside the bodice of her dress. She hooked her wicker basket containing the matchboxes over the crook of her arm as she set off to find a pitch. She felt bad about pawning the doll, so wouldn't be standing outside the Sampson shop today for fear she would be asked questions about it. She couldn't in all honesty pretend to be loving the doll when it was now on a shelf at Mr Goodman's shop.

She set up on her new pitch quite early morning, a good twenty-minute walk away from home. Custom had been brisk as the snow had now begun to clear away, turning to a dusky grey slush underfoot where people had trampled over it. Puddles of ice-cold water seeped into the soles of her boots and she blew on her gloveless hands.

Thankfully, trade was quite brisk at this pitch and a gentleman had even taken pity on her, dropping an extra couple of pennies into her palm. But then as she served one elderly man, she placed her basket on the pavement as she searched for change, to turn around and discover it missing while her back was turned.

Someone had stolen it!

Fear gripped her heart. She could have wept as there were still a few boxes of matches that she could have sold there, but at least her takings and the money from Mr Goodman were in the little leather purse on a string that she'd tucked into the bodice of her dress before arriving at the pitch. Imagine if that had gone too? All her hard work would have been for nothing. She'd have been devastated. Holding her horizontal hand to her forehead, she squinted her eyes as she scanned the busy street to see if there was any sign of who might have robbed her, but all she saw were people of all classes milling around. No one who looked like someone who'd have made off with her basket.

She was just about to set off back home, now with no basket and minus the remaining boxes of matches, when a young lad wearing a threadbare jacket and trousers and flat cap, came running towards her with the basket. So that was the thief, the bloomin' cheek of it! And now he was coming back for her takings too.

She gritted her teeth and put up both fists in a boxing stance. 'Don't you dare!' she accused. 'Don't you bleedin' dare!'

The lad frowned and looked confused for a moment, then his features relaxed as he smiled broadly. 'It weren't me what took your basket, miss. It was one of the Wilson Gang.'

'Wilson gang?' She angled her head to one side as she studied the lad before her.

'Yes. I saw one of them scarpering away with it as you served a gent just now. So I ran after him. I'm fast on me feet, see!' He beamed as though proud of his achievement. 'I wrestled the varmint to the ground and got it back for you.'

Tears filled Angeline's eyes. 'I…I don't know what to say…' she said, totally overtaken by the boy's kindness.

'You could say thank you, I suppose!' He chuckled.

'Of course I should.' She fumbled with the purse around her neck.

He held up a vertical, grubby palm. 'Certainly not, miss. I'm not after your money. I'm just glad to be of assistance.'

'Oh?' She replaced her purse in the bodice of her dress, so it remained out of sight. 'I'm sorry, I'm just so used to people doing bad things, especially around this place.'

The lad cocked her a cheeky grin. 'Aye, there's a lot of bad about but I find most folk beneath it all are good sorts. A lot steal from necessity and want.'

'Well, I don't,' said Angeline, she swallowed

hard. 'I mean I could have like today for instance as my Pa has left us all. Gone off with another woman and Ma is finding it hard to cope. But instead, I've taken a Christmas present I was given to the pawn shop and here I am on the street...'

'Selling matches,' the lad said, finishing her sentence for her.

'Yes. I don't want to deprive someone else.'

'And it's right you are, my dear. Now then, you look like you could do with a warm by the fireside to me. I've never seen you around the Old Nichol area before. Are you far from home?'

She nodded. 'It's about a twenty-minute walk. You see, my usual pitch is near the shop of the person who gave me that gift for Christmas and I feel ever so guilty for pawning it.'

His expressive dark eyes softened. 'What was it then, love?' he tilted his head.

'A porcelain doll. An angel doll. Something I'd like to have kept for myself. I don't play with dolls any more, but this one was different, it was more ornamental.'

'That was very generous of you. Look, come with me...'

She hesitated for a moment. 'I don't know if I should.' She frowned. After all, she didn't know this lad from Adam and her mother had told her to be wary of strangers. But then again, he wasn't far off her age and he had already helped her and wanted to help her further.

'You'll be safe with me, honestly. We can warm

ourselves by the fireside and Ma has made some cakes today.'

Angeline's mouth watered at the thought of a tasty treat. And after all, the lad must be all right, he'd just returned her basket to her with nothing missing. 'Thank you, I'll come with you,' she said softly.

He nodded eagerly and smiled. 'Then come this way...'

He led her across the busy thoroughfare, dodging a horse and cart and a couple of barrows until they were safely on the other side. Then down a narrow alleyway in between some shops and a rabbit warren of narrow lanes, until they arrived at some squalid-looking houses where ragged children played and a mangy-looking cat sat on a window sill, preening itself.

'This is ours,' he declared. 'We've cellar rooms.'

Angeline had never been in a cellar room before, she looked at the uneven series of stone steps leading to them.

'It's all right. Ma keeps the place spick and span,' he said as if he was proud of his mother's achievement. 'Come on,' he beckoned with his hand as he urged her to follow him down the cellar steps. With some trepidation, she gingerly followed after him being mindful of keeping her balance. This wasn't what she'd been expecting at all when he said he'd take her back home with him to sit in front of the fire. All right, she'd not been expecting a palace or anything, but somehow she hadn't envisaged a cellar-dwelling.

'It's all right,' he said quietly. 'You'll like me Ma.'

It wasn't his Ma she was worried about, it was what she'd find when she stepped inside. But she was pleasantly surprised as the first thing she spotted was the warm, welcoming fire blazing away in the hearth at the far end of the room. There was little furniture, just like at her own home. A table with a couple of chairs in the centre of the room. An old armchair and mismatched settee. On the mantel was a wooden clock that ticked very loudly, showing the time at twenty-five minutes past twelve. Gosh, she'd been out all this time selling matches, she hadn't even realised.

The smell of vanilla, cinnamon and some sort of fruit, drifted towards her and she sniffed the air.

'See, I told you Ma was baking today!' the lad announced proudly.

Then before Angeline had the chance to reply, a middle-aged woman with her hair up in a bun came heading towards them. She wasn't thin and gaunt like her own ma, oh no. This lady was full-figured and she wore a clean white apron over her flowered dress. Angeline noticed the woman had some sort of white powder dotted on her face and some on her hands. Then she realised, of course, it was from the flour she'd used for baking.

When she noticed her son had brought someone home with him, the woman's face split into a wide grin. 'Well hello, young lady,' she greeted. 'Thomas has brought you home with him to taste one of my cakes, has he?'

Angeline smiled and nodded. At least she now knew the lad's name. 'Yes, missus.'

'I'd like it if you told me your name before you taste one of my offerings,' she chuckled.

'It's Angeline Barker.'

'And I'm Mrs Featherstone. Now come along, you look perished. Take that chair by the fire, dear, and hand me your shawl.'

Angeline did as told and she laid her basket down near the hearth and seated herself in the armchair while Thomas looked on.

'Good. Now you can take the weight off your feet while I brew up a cuppa for us all. You like tea, don't you?'

'Oh yes, missus. Yes, please.' Angeline could hardly believe the kindness of the woman.

When his mother had gone, Thomas said, 'You can call me Tommy, everyone else does. It's only my ma what calls me Thomas.'

Angeline nodded. She thought she understood.

After a few minutes, Mrs Featherstone returned with a tray containing three brown mugs with a plate of sliced cake on it. 'It's a sultana cake. Hope you like it, Angeline.'

She nodded. 'I expect I will.' In truth, she'd never tasted it before but she had tried currant buns, which she figured might be something similar.

Mrs Featherstone handed her a plate with a slice of cake on which she noticed had been generously spread with butter, causing her mouth to water at the mere thought of taking a morsel.

'I'll put your mug of tea down near the hearth. Do you take sugar?'

'No, thanks.' The truth here was that her family rarely had enough money to purchase a bag of sugar, so more often than not, they went without it in their cups of tea, so her palate was quite used to unsugared tea. Tommy, she noticed shovelled a spoonful in his cup and stirred it well, while Mrs Featherstone, herself, did not take any. The woman sat herself down on the settee beside her son.

As they settled down, Angeline waited for someone to take a bite of their cake before giving herself permission to take a nibble. It was Tommy who got down to it first, so Angeline did the same, closing her eyes as she tasted the cinnamon and she thought there was a hint of ginger there too and the plump, juicy sultanas tasted heavenly. The butter too was slightly salted which one might not have thought a good combination with the sweetness involved, but in this case, it was.

Angelina's eyes flicked open to see Mrs Featherstone smiling at her. 'It's good to see someone enjoy one of my cakes, it gives me a lot of pleasure,' she said, as she eyed her up. ''Course, Thomas is well used to my cakes. He often gets to try them before anyone else.' Then she went on to explain, 'He's got three older brothers, see. His pa passed on a few years ago, but my lads, well they went to work and took over their father's business. He was a costermonger. They've taken over his round.'

Angeline wrinkled her nose in confusion.

'Don't you know what a costermonger is?' said Tommy with great surprise.

'No, I'm not really sure.' She shook her head.

'I can guarantee you do know you just don't know the name of what they are!' He grinned at her.

'Well, put the girl out of her misery,' said his ma.

'A costermonger is a person who sells fruit and veg. Often around the streets. Our Billy, he takes out the donkey and cart and sells to housewives and such around the houses. Eddie and Reggie, well they have a market stall.'

'Oh, I see,' said Angeline. 'You're right. I did know of those sorts of people, I just didn't know the name for them.'

'There are lots of coster folk living in this area,' explained Mrs Featherstone. 'They're hardworking people but sometimes we get a bad name as some are into dog fighting in the pubs, gambling and that sort of thing. We live cheek to jowl around these parts and while some fight amongst themselves, any strangers who come to the area to interfere, then we stick together. I'm not meaning you of course, dear.'

Tommy winked at her. She hadn't for a moment thought his mother was referring to her as "one of those strangers" but she supposed she was a stranger of sorts.

'So, then, tell me, Angeline. Where do you live,

luvvy, and what were you doing out in this cold weather this morning?'

Angeline hesitated before speaking, she wasn't one for telling people her business but she figured Mrs Featherstone and her son were good sorts. 'I live near the match factory.'

'At Bow?' Mrs Featherstone blinked.

'Yes. And I sell matches, so that's why I was out in the cold this morning when your Tommy, er I mean Thomas found me.'

'Yes, one of the Wilson gang ran off with her basket of matches and I chased him until he dropped it and gave it to me.'

'Well done, son!' said his mother with great admiration in her eyes.

'But you're a fair distance from Bow, over this way?' Mrs Featherstone narrowed her eyes.

Angeline felt her face grow hot and she hoped it hadn't gone red. 'I...I...'

But before she had the chance to explain about the angel doll, Tommy butted in. 'Could we have another slice of cake, Ma, please?'

His mother nodded and headed off to the scullery to fetch some more, all the while going there muttering, 'Where do you put it all, Thomas?'

Where indeed? Angeline realised the lad hadn't even finished his first piece yet, she'd noticed him removing it from the plate and hiding it behind a cushion on his chair.

'What's going on?' she frowned, not liking the

idea that his ma had baked a perfectly good cake and he was deceiving her in some way.

'Sssh!' he whispered, putting his index finger to his lips. 'It's for a pal of mine who's living out on the street. Bobby Swindler's his name.'

Feeling confused, Angeline whispered, 'But why is it such a secret? Can't you tell your ma?'

'No,' said Tommy.

'But whyever not?'

'He's hiding from his uncle, who when he'll find him, will give him a right good leathering.'

'Has he done something wrong, then?'

'Oh no. Bobby only has to look at his uncle twice to get a leathering. The man's a beast. He's been forcing him up chimneys and all sorts. Even though it was outlawed years ago, he'd think nothing about sending him up a chimney in one of those big fancy houses. He's a master chimney sweep, see.'

Angeline pursed her lips, pensively, before shaking her head. 'How awful.'

'The lad is petrified. He once got stuck up a narrow chimney breast as he's getting too big to climb up them anyhow and he froze. Do you know what that cruel uncle of his did and all?'

Angeline shrugged her shoulders.

'He stuck a pin in the soles of his feet to cause him pain and make him move sharpish. Not a little pin like a dressmaker uses neither, but one of the long lady's hat pins!'

Angeline's hands flew to her face in horror. 'If I'd

known that I'd have given Bobby my slice of cake too!'

'You weren't to know, but what you can do, when me ma comes back with cake for us...will you take a second slice and save it for Bobby?'

Angeline smiled. 'Of course I will.' She was more than glad to give it away as she felt sated after the first slice and the cup of tea. She couldn't bear to think of a young lad suffering like that.

'Just pretend to eat it and when me ma's not looking, hide it behind you. Then later slip it into your basket.'

She nodded, realising that old saying of her mother's was perfectly true. "There's always someone worse off than yourself."

After staying a while longer to chat with Mrs Featherstone, Angeline made her excuses to leave.

'It was very nice meeting you, Angeline. Thomas will see you safely back home, won't you, Thomas?'

Tommy nodded eagerly.

Thankfully, Angeline had hidden that extra slice in her basket and she'd placed her neckerchief on top of it so it remained hidden, she guessed Tommy must have slipped his into his jacket pocket.

As they were about to leave, Mrs Featherstone grabbed her arm and for one awful moment, she thought the woman knew about the cake, but then she said, 'Any time you're passing this way, do call in. You're more than welcome, dear.'

Angeline nodded her thanks and left in Tommy's wake.

***

'Phew! That was a close one there,' Tommy said when they'd reached the top of the steps and were ready to leave the area. 'I thought for a moment Ma had caught hold of you to see what was in your basket.'

'I know,' said Angeline. 'I kept the cake hidden under my neckerchief though. 'But I still don't understand why you can't tell your ma as she might help out or take him in.'

'I know, I did wonder meself at one time but Bobby swore I'm not to tell the adults in case word gets back to his uncle and he gets another thrashing. As it is, he'd prefer to sleep rough than be forced up another searing hot chimney breast.'

Angeline could well understand that. 'I wish I could help out more but we're on our uppers as it is with Pa leaving us in the lurch like that. Not that he's much good anyhow. He's a chimney sweep an' all but he don't sweep that many chimneys as he's in the pub a lot after that barmaid.'

Tommy narrowed his eyes. 'A chimneysweep you say? What's his name?'

Angeline could see that Tommy was wondering if he was Bobby's uncle but she'd never heard mention of the name and he just used brushes, no boys. 'Bertie Barker. You heard of him?'

To her relief, Tommy shook his head. 'This fella is named Arnold Swindler.' He paused for a moment before saying, 'Please don't tell anyone this information about him or his nephew. Else Bobby might end up in a lot of trouble. I swear he'll kill him if he catches him this time.'

'This time? There was another?' She shielded her eyes as the sun had now broken through the clouds. 'And don't worry, of course, I won't breathe a word.'

'Yes, Bobby's run away before and his uncle always catches him but this time I've found a good hiding place for him and it's the longest he's ever kept away for.'

'Where is this place?' Seeing Tommy's troubled gaze, she added, 'Sorry, I shouldn't have asked.'

He touched her arm. 'Yes, best you don't know, love. Now come on, let's get you back home. I'll have that slice of cake off you when you get near home in case anyone spots you handing it over and tells Ma.'

She nodded. As she gazed around at the squalid dilapidated dwellings, some of which had windows stuffed with newspaper and rags, a shiver coursed the length of her spine at what was going on with Bobby and that uncle of his. Arnold Swindler made Bertie Barker look like he was a good father to his own children, and for him to do that, she figured the man must be rotten to the core!

Chapter Six

Angeline said her goodbyes to Tommy at the entrance to Christmas Alley and he promised he'd keep in touch, just as she was about to turn into it, a voice cried out. "Miss Barker!"

Tommy had already left her side and was sauntering along the street in the direction of home with his hands stuffed in his pockets.

Her head whipped around to be met with the towering figure of Mr Goodman. 'I've been looking for you,' he said with a big smile on his face. 'Can you call into the shop later?'

She nodded, wondering what was going on. 'Can't you tell me now, please?' She'd been on her feet all morning and the last thing she needed was a trek over to the pawn shop after the walk back and forth to the Old Nichol area.

'Very well. It's the doll...' he said excitedly. 'I think it may be quite rare. I shall have to check to see if I can find out how many were made.'

At that moment, Eliza made an appearance, her eyes shining and cheeks flushed as though she'd just arrived from an assignation with George. 'What was that, Mr Goodman?'

'Oh hello, dear. I was just telling your sister that

the doll she brought in earlier this morning might be quite rare and I am going to check how many were made.'

'We don't care how many were made though,' said Eliza as her chin protruded, 'we just want to pawn this one!'

'I know and I understand your impatience, dear girl, but the less of the dolls that were made, the more valuable they become,' he said as Eliza's eyes widened—she was obviously seeing falling pennies before her very eyes.

'There is a great demand for such craftmanship. It's my feeling that this particular doll might have been crafted by Olivier Marsaud.'

'But how do you know that, Mr Goodman?' Angeline tilted her head to one side, curious now.

'It's marked on the back of the doll "Made in France",' he said. Angeline nodded, this she already knew from the owner of the toy shop. 'Just below that in gilt paint in very small initials that are almost invisible to the naked eye, it displays the initials OM. If you come to the shop later, I'll show you...' he said with mounting excitement.

'We'll come right now!' butted in Eliza as she nudged her sister's elbow.

Oh no, this was the last thing Angeline needed but then again if the doll was valuable, it might be worth making the effort to walk over to the shop.

***

'You see, most manufacturers of this sort leave their mark of some kind on a doll...' Mr Goodman explained later inside the shop.

Angeline and Eliza drew nearer as he removed a box from the shelf behind him and placed it on the window counter in front of him. Then he opened it and removed the tissue paper and laid the doll on the counter. 'These marks are sometimes to be found on the head, shoulder, neck, or the bottom of the foot. Some of these dolls come with a certificate of authenticity, which can help greatly with their identification. But in this case, there appears to be no certificate, unless the person who gave it to you has one?' He looked at Angeline who shrugged her shoulders at him.

'Sorry, I don't know.'

'Maybe you can find out?' He looked at her with raised eyebrows over the top of his silver-rimmed spectacles.

She found herself nodding but doubted she'd ask Mrs Sampson. It would be so impertinent of her to question a gift. Besides, she wouldn't want the woman to know she had pawned the doll or even that she'd consider selling it, that just wouldn't do.

'But how come you didn't notice the initials when my sister first brought it to the shop?' Eliza asked through narrowed eyes.

Mr Goodman smiled. 'Ah, it's because as I said to you earlier, it was almost invisible to the naked eye, I used a jeweller's loupe to check it out.'

Eliza frowned. 'Huh?'

'Pardon?' Angeline corrected her sister. 'It's rude

of you to say "Huh?".'

'Never mind about that, I want to know what a loupe is!' Eliza said enthusiastically.

'There's no mystery about it,' laughed Mr Goodman. 'It's a small eyeglass a jeweller uses to study a piece of jewellery in fine detail. Like to see if it has a hallmark to prove it's real silver or gold, that sort of thing.'

'Oh, I see,' said Eliza smiling now.

'Now then,' said Mr Goodman, 'you can both try the loupe or eyeglass to see for yourselves.'

'Oh can we, Mr Goodman!' Eliza said excitedly clasping her hands together almost as if in prayer.

You'd swear it was her doll, not mine! Thought Angeline.

As if realising this, Mr Goodman offered the loupe to Angeline first, showing her how to place it to her eye and explaining what to look for. 'See there,' he said softly, 'at the back of the doll's neck are the initials OM.'

'Oh yes,' said Angeline, excited herself now.

'And then further down at the doll's lower back, there is a registration number. See that too?'

She brought her gaze further down. 'Yes, I do. It says 3150H.'

'That is correct.'

She removed the glass from her eye and handed it to him. 'But what does that number mean?'

'It's a registration number. Now if I can trace it, I can find out how many were made and then find out if it's rare or not and how much it might be worth.'

"'Ere, hang on a minute!' said Eliza as she narrowed her eyes with suspicion, 'what do you want out of this?'

Mr Goodman held up his palms as if in defence. 'I'm not after anything. Usually, I'd take a certain percentage of what's owed to me but in your case...' his face reddened, 'I've heard all about what your father's done to you all, and quite frankly, it sickens me.'

Angeline swallowed a lump in her throat, she didn't want anyone to feel sorry for them. 'Eliza, you take a look with the eyeglass now,' she said, passing it to her to break the painful moment and change the topic of conversation.

Eliza accepted the loupe as though grateful too for the awkward moment to pass. She placed it to her eye and lifted the doll to study it carefully, then removing the eyeglass and placing it on the counter, she smiled. 'Thank you, Mr Goodman. When can you let us know any more about the doll?'

'Hopefully, in a day or two when I've visited my friend with it. He has an antique shop a couple of miles away from here. He knows a lot about porcelain dolls as his wife collects them. You never know, once we establish its true worth, he may wish to purchase it from you as a little gift for her.'

Angeline felt her heart sink. Deep down, she wished to keep the doll as she'd never been given anything so beautiful in all her life, but needs must she supposed.

***

On the journey back home Angeline was subdued.

'What's the matter with you?' Eliza wanted to know. 'You look like yer've dropped a sovereign and found a farthing!'

In a manner of speaking, it felt like she had. She let out a long sigh. 'I suppose it's because I feel bad for accepting that beautiful doll from Mrs Sampson and now getting rid of it!' She sulked.

'Aw come on, it's not as if it's for a bad thing. You're doing it to help out the family, to put food on the table and such.'

Angeline realised her sister made a good point.

'I suppose I could explain the situation to Mrs Sampson,' she said, placing her index finger on her chin in contemplation.

'No, don't do that!' yelled Eliza.

Angeline frowned. 'But why not?'

'I'll tell you why not, because she might think you don't appreciate her gift and ask for it back. Folk are funny like that.'

'But I was always taught at Sunday school that honesty is the best policy.'

'Not in this case. Keep quiet about it, at least until the doll is sold. Then you can tell her afterwards when there's not a cat in hell's chance she can get it back.'

Every step Angeline took towards home now felt heavy, as heavy as her heart. She wished there was an easy solution to this, but there was none that she could see.

***

The following morning, Angeline was out selling matches again at the same pitch. It felt even colder than the previous day. She hoped she'd see Tommy again but there was no sign of him. This time she kept her eyes firmly fixed on her basket full of matchboxes, either keeping it over the crook of her arm or if she had to lay it down, it was at her feet, where she could keep an eye on it. There was no sign of anyone with fast fingers either and she wondered how fast that Wilson gang member must have been yesterday for her not to have even laid eyes on him.

This morning, trade was slow. Yesterday had been a busy morning with it being a Monday, the start of the business trading week. In the distance, she could see a couple of women trying to sell flowers. Not the best pitch for that she guessed. If it were her, she'd use her noddle and turn up outside the theatres in the evening, or even in Victoria Park on a Sunday afternoon when gentlemen were out walking with their sweethearts.

A coach and horses thundered past, startling her and causing her to step further back on the pavement. This was such a busy thoroughfare for all sorts of vehicles. Her fingers were now numb and blue with the cold and she half hoped Tommy would suddenly show up and take her back to his house for a warm. Then she remembered his mother had told her to call at any time but she felt she didn't know the woman well enough to do so on her own, and the fact she knew Tommy's secret about his friend wouldn't help either. Best not go there alone as if the woman asked her any awkward questions, she'd find it hard to lie, even if she couldn't tell her where the poor lad was hidden.

She'd collected a few pennies so far and her stomach was growling with hunger so she decided to purchase a hot jacket potato with butter from a stall across the road. She'd use that to warm up her hands for a while and when it had cooled a little, then she'd eat it.

She was just about to cross the road when a strong arm grabbed her from behind. Startled, she turned to see her father there swaying back and forth, smelling strongly of alcohol. 'Hey, what are you doing here?' He asked as he stuffed his hands in his pockets.

'N...nothing...' She lied. This was one time when she felt justified. She didn't want him to know she'd been selling matches here for a very good reason.

'Don't give me that, girl!' His eyes enlarged and he appeared to snarl at her.

'I...I...I'm telling the truth.'

'You never were much of a liar.' He grabbed her basket roughly from her grasp and peered inside. 'Selling matches, were you?'

She nodded, her mouth agape.

'Good girl,' he said and to her surprise, he ruffled her hair. 'Now hand over your takings, my throat is right parched.'

Not blooming likely, she thought. *Not for you to spend my hard-earned money in that pub across the road.*

The pennies were in her purse around her neck which he didn't know about.

'Come on, darlin', hand over your money to your dear Daddy!'

Her eyes enlarged with fear. And then he dropped the basket, and taking her by the shoulders, began to shake her roughly, causing passersby to stare and wonder what was going on but no one did anything.

***

Angeline's teeth rattled in her head as her father carried on shaking her. Every bone in her body seemed to ache but she was determined not to tell him where those precious pennies were. She needed them to help feed the family.

Suddenly, he released her from his grasp and she tumbled backwards onto the pavement. He stood towering over her, and to her horror, began to unbuckle his leather belt from his trousers. That could only mean one thing—a leathering. He'd never so much as laid a finger on her before. Michael, yes, when he'd been a bit younger, he'd belted him a few times when he'd been defiant or got himself into trouble. But these days, Michael was as tall as him and strong and muscular since working in the butchery business. He reckoned it was from carting around sides of beef and walking the streets making deliveries that kept him so fit.

'Damn you, girl!' her father said holding his belt aloft as though it were a whip.

Angeline struggled to pull herself onto her feet but slipped on the slush and as she heard a crack as the leather belt whipped through the air, she closed her eyes tightly shut, clasped her hands together and prayed the buckle itself didn't make contact with her.

But she waited and there was nothing.

Gingerly, she opened one eye and then the other. Her father was gone. It was then she noticed him entering the pub on the opposite side of the road.

What on earth was the matter with him? He'd never shown such violence to her before but then again, maybe he'd never drunk so much alcohol before either. Her mother often said: "When the beer is in, the wit is out!" Which proved to be true in her father's case.

Brushing her clothing down with the palm of her hand, she then retrieved her basket thinking it would be best if she got herself out of here. She couldn't bear it if her father attacked her again when he left that pub.

Breathing heavily, she walked unsteadily along the road in the direction of home and then she heard a familiar voice cry out: 'Angeline, wait!'

Turning to look behind her, she was relieved

to see Tommy running to catch up with her, his breath coming out like puffs of steam from a train engine as it hit the cold frosty air.

'What's the matter with you?' he asked when he finally caught up with her.

'It's my f...father...' she sniffed, on the verge of tears now.

'Aw, are you still upset he's left you all?' he asked as he draped a comforting arm around her shoulders.

'No, it's not that,' she said in barely a whisper. 'He just caught me with my basket of matches and demanded my takings from me.'

'What on earth?' Tommy wrinkled his nose. 'He's got a flamin' cheek that one. After leaving you all in the lurch like that.'

'That's not all though. I've got my takings, which weren't much this morning, around my neck in a purse. I refused to show him where they were and he began to shake me. It was horrible, Tommy.' She began to sob now. 'Then...he shook me so hard that I fell backwards and he removed his leather belt to...'

'The bleedin' beast!' yelled Tommy. 'Why, I'd like to catch up with him and give him a leathering he'd never forget. Did he hurt you with his belt?'

'No,' she shook her head. 'I tried to get up again and slipped on the slush. I closed my eyes expecting a leathering and when there was none, I opened them and he'd gone.'

'Thought better of it I suppose. That's

something at least. No doubt people were watching him.'

'They were.'

'Come on, you're not going home in that state, I'm taking you back to mine and I suggest you get a different pitch tomorrow. Or if you do want to return here, arrange for me to stand with you.'

'You'd do that for me?' She blinked.

'Sure I would.' He cocked her a cheeky grin.

It was good to know she had a friend like Tommy.

Chapter Seven

'He did what?' said Michael later that afternoon when Angeline told her brother all about the incident with their father.

'I'm sure he was going to belt me one and he shook me as well.'

'Strange he should do that because he saw you selling matches, Angeline.'

'No, that wasn't the reason. He was after my takings.'

'That bleedin' figures. What a swine. Maybe it's best you stop selling them, love,' he said with a great deal of sympathy in his blue eyes.

'I'd rather not as sometimes I can make some good money. Some gentlemen take pity on me and give me extra.'

'I know you don't mind selling them because everyone else here used to moan about making matchboxes and that's why you decided to do it, but I think maybe you should go to the man you buy the matches from and ask if you can assemble matchboxes again. That way you can stay in the warm and there's no chance of running into Pa again.'

Angeline thought for a moment. 'But there's

always a chance of that, Michael. Even when we're at home. I could be home alone and he might come here. At least out there, I can find a different pitch. I've made a new friend.'

'Oh?'

'A boy a bit older than me called Tommy Featherstone. He lives around the Old Nichol area with his mother and brothers. He's offered to come with me to sell matches.'

'If he's offering I suppose, but that's a good walk away from here, love.' He ruffled her hair. 'I reckon you'd be better off staying local.'

'But I don't make so much money here as it's a quieter area.'

'Hmmm, that's a dilemma I suppose.'

Angeline bit into her lip. 'Please don't tell Ma, will you? I don't want to worry her. She worries enough as it is, me going out early mornings.'

'All right,' smiled Michael. 'I can see the sense of that. I think I need to have a word with Eliza though, she's the one who needs a flipping good shaking, not you. She's bone idle. She could have helped more when you were all making matchboxes together.'

Michael was right. If her sister pulled her weight instead of spooning with George, life would be a lot easier for them all, she barely even helped with the housework.

***

Later that day, Angeline headed off to the match factory which was a few streets over from their home at a place called Fairfield Road in Bow. In the distance, loud and proud was a tall stack which stood out. The smoke that belched from that place made Angeline's stomach heave as it smelled strongly of sulphur from the matchmaking process. She was hoping she might have a word with someone about making matchboxes from home. She had no intention of not selling matches herself as Michael had suggested, but this assembling matchboxes palaver was a sideline the whole family might help with, even the little ones. It was a task they all hated undertaking as it was so fiddly and a matchbox could easily be ruined in the process, but it was a way to stay in the warm even if it was a long, laborious task. It provided a regular, if small income too.

Her intention today was to see one of the sweaters called Mr Arkwright. A sweater was like a go-between for the bosses and the homeworkers taken on by the company. He was the man Ma had previously been to when she'd left the factory with her bad chest and persistent cough. He'd taken pity on her and had given her some homework assembling matchboxes but unfortunately, she'd fallen behind with it. Angeline was hoping he'd take pity on her today if she explained this time it wouldn't just be her Ma's responsibility but her own and her siblings' too.

As she approached the red brick building, she glanced up at the large wrought iron gates and the clock that was set into the building itself, beckoning the factory workers inside. The bosses at Bryant and May were hard taskmasters expecting the women and girls to work long shifts with little time for breaks. They came into regular contact with a hazardous substance called phosphorus in those matches. It was rumoured there were pools of glowing vomit around the area that showed up, particularly at night time as phosphorus glowed in the dark.

Her eyes fixed on an attendant at the gate, so she asked him where she might locate Mr Arkwright.

'He's not here at the moment, miss,' said the middle-aged man who had bushy sideburns and a twirled moustache. 'One of the others, Mr Rutherford, is around here somewhere. I can send someone to look for him, if you like. Other than that, you'll have to come back first thing in the morning and queue with all the others.'

That's the last thing she wanted, that queue could stretch a long way, and she needed help right now.

'Well, if you could fetch Mr Rutherford for me, that would be most kind of you.' She smiled at the man who returned her smile. That was a relief as some of the men who manned the gate were difficult sorts. She watched as he sent a young lad in the direction of the main factory building and she waited patiently.

Presently, she noticed a sturdy, pot-bellied gentleman come striding slowly towards her. He was well dressed in a brown tweed suit with an open jacket and brown waistcoat. On his head was a bowler hat.

'Hello, young lady,' he said. 'I've just been told you're looking for me?'

'Yes, sir. You see, I already work for Bryant and May selling matches on the street and my mother, Mavis Barker, used to work at the factory until she came down with a chronic chest complaint.'

'I see,' said Mr Rutherford as he scratched his chin as if wondering what this young girl wanted from him. 'So, how might I help?'

'Ma used to assemble matchboxes from home when she left here, but as she was ill for so long, slipped behind with her work and was given no more. Now we find ourselves in a bad place as Pa has left us all, I was just wondering if I might be able to buy the stuff needed so I can make them with the help of my brother and sisters instead of our mother?'

The sweater stared at her long and hard. 'And have you money to pay for all the equipment? Bryant and May isn't a charity you know.'

She nodded enthusiastically at him. 'Yes, sir. I've been working hard for a long time selling matches, I reckon I could afford it.'

'You'll need cardboard, of course, paste and hemp string and so on...'

'Yes, sir. I understand.'

'You'll get paid two and a half pennies per gross of boxes made, understood?'

She smiled. 'Thank you, sir.'

'Don't want no slacking, mind you.' He wagged a chubby finger in her direction. 'You'll need to keep up with it. Making those boxes might keep you up well into the night.'

Angeline felt like she could have kissed the man. Their problems weren't over by a long chalk, but this would really help the family finances. She gave him her address and he returned to the factory and came back with the necessary equipment for her.

'Next time though, you'll have to queue up with the rest of them,' he said but then he winked at her and she knew that beneath that hard-looking exterior was a heart of gold.

It wouldn't be practical for her to queue up every morning to collect the cardboard and glue and whatever, but she could send Eliza in her place when she needed to be at her pitch. Yes, it was all going to work out nicely indeed. What with Michael's earnings from the butcher shop and her earnings from her match work, they needn't starve and it would help to keep a roof over all of their heads and food in their bellies. That rotten father of theirs had a lot to answer for.

***

When Angeline placed the matchbox-making equipment down on the living room table, Eliza groaned. 'I hope you're not expecting me to help with that!' she complained. 'I had enough of trying to help Ma the last time—it's so damn fiddly!'

Angeline gritted her teeth in frustration. 'Well, I've still got matches to sell. Unless you want to take over from me and I'll make the boxes instead, that way I can stay out of the cold.'

Eliza sighed. 'Oh, all right then but Sammy and Joanna will have to help and Ma and Michael.'

'No!' yelled Angeline, surprising herself with the fierce tone of her own voice, causing Eliza to stare at her.

'Whyever not?' she asked after an awkward pause.

'It's all right to ask Sammy and Joanna when they come home from school but they can't be at it all evening like Ma used to be. And Ma isn't all that well so you'll have to see how she's feeling. As for Michael, isn't he always so tired out after being on his feet all day at the butcher shop? Heaving heavy carcasses around, standing serving customers and then taking out deliveries? No! You are to be the main worker. And another thing...'

Her sister's mouth popped open and snapped shut again.

'I've got you the equipment to do the job and I know you know how to make them as you did help after a fashion for a while when Ma was doing it until you started running after George, but from now on, you are to collect what's needed from the factory, not me. I have enough to do as it is.'

Eliza nodded slowly, her face looking blank now as though she were in some kind of shock after the way her sister had just spoken to her. Angeline had given her no choice in the matter and she was backed up against the wall as if she refused then she would look bad.

Hearing a cough behind them, the girls' heads whipped around.

'I thought I heard raised voices,' Ma said quietly in a husky tone which Angeline guessed was the result of her persistent bouts of coughing.

'Sorry, Ma. We were just discussing something,' Angeline smiled warmly at their mother. 'Come and sit by the fire. I hope we didn't wake you.'

'No, you didn't.' Ma headed tentatively towards her favourite armchair nearest the hearth. 'I've just been lying there on the bed wondering how we're going to cope.'

'Now don't you worry about that. Eliza has come up with a marvellous idea that should help us through a lean time.' Angeline shot her sister a warning glance as though she wanted her to go along with the white lie.

Eliza smiled and kneeling near their mother, took her hand. 'Yes, Ma. I came up with the idea of making matchboxes again, just like you used to. Only this time you won't need to help. I'll do most of it and Sammy and Joanna can help when they're around. Though of course, I won't keep them up past their bedtimes as they have school in the mornings.'

'There's good you are to me,' said Ma with a tear in her eyes.

That was just typical of Eliza taking the credit for the matchbox-making idea but Angeline had been canny as that's what she expected. Eliza loved revelling in the glory and being made out to be a little angel when it was Angeline who was really. If she hadn't walked over to the factory and asked to see one of the sweaters then her sister would be doing the exact same thing tomorrow to help —nothing whatsoever. But for the time being, she was more than happy for her sister to claim the credit for Michael's idea. She just hoped now she'd stick to her word in future about queueing up with the other girls and women to collect the necessary equipment and then to get on with it.

'I'll go and make some tea for us all, shall I Ma?' Angeline studied her mother's drawn and tired-looking face.

Ma nodded. 'That would be lovely.' Then the tears began to roll down her cheeks. 'What would I do without you girls, and Michael too? You're ever such a support to me.'

Angeline now knelt in front of their mother, taking her free hand as Eliza still held the other. 'Ma, we're always here for you. You'll never lose us, ever,' she said as her sister nodded in agreement.

Their mother looked up. 'But how did you manage to buy the cardboard and glue to make the boxes?' She sniffed loudly.

This was something Eliza could not answer, she looked at her sister for a prompt.

Swallowing, Angeline said, 'I had some money I made this past couple of days from selling matches, so I put it to good use. I know I could have used it to buy more food but I thought I'd help Eliza get started when she suggested the idea.'

Eliza smiled at her. She needed to keep the girl on her side if she was to get any work out of her.

Ma looked old these days, so frail and hunched up. Not the strong, vibrant mother they'd all known a few years back. Working at the match factory had taken its toll and they were still living in the shadow of that place.

***

Warily, Angeline stood in the same pitch again the following morning but this time Tommy was by her side. She felt guilty keeping the lad away from other things he might be doing as she knew he helped his mother by chopping sticks for firewood and collecting coal from the merchant on a wooden barrow. But this morning, he claimed to have clear so she was more than glad of his help. He was a good salesperson too as he shouted out:

'Get yer best quality matches here! Genuine Bryant and May safety matches!'

'Come along, ladies and gents. Don't be mean, don't be shy, step right up and buy! Buy! Buy!'

He did seem to generate extra custom for her, and for some reason, the customers thought the pair made a cute couple so they ended up with some extras. One lady dipped her gloved hand into her basket, presenting them both with an orange each, and a couple of gents gave them a penny or two.

Thankfully, there was no sign of Angeline's father and she was grateful for that. She could do without him throwing his weight around. In any case, Tommy said he'd be prepared for him if he appeared on the scene and started on her. His brother Billy, the one who went around the streets with his cart, was at home this morning trying to repair a broken wheel on it, so if needs be he'd run and fetch him. This morning, Angeline had no fears of that kind. Besides, people were beginning to know her now and where she stood with her wicker basket of matches.

The only concern she had was if Eliza was getting on with her work to help the family finances. She'd find out soon enough when she returned home. Sammy and Joanna were back at school today after the Christmas holidays. Angeline had left school herself a couple of years ago. She'd loved it there but girls usually finished their education at ten years old and boys at fourteen, which she thought most unfair. She'd enjoyed school. Her favourite subjects had been English and Mathematics. Most of her friends saw nothing more for themselves than wanting to leave and then help their mothers around the home until a suitable husband came along, well that wasn't for her. She wanted more out of life.

'Come and get yer matches here!' Shouted Tommy beside her, breaking her out of her reverie.

She smiled at him.

'Don't think we'll do much more here, the golden hour is over...' he said sadly.

She glanced at the time on the church clock just

down the road. It was now gone ten o'clock and most passing trade of people going to work had been over some time ago. However, she did know that around lunchtime it picked up again.

She nodded at him. 'I guess you're right, Tommy.'

'Come on, we'll go back to mine again and you can meet Billy. I'm going to take some food over to Bobby, so if yer get the chance take extra from Ma again. I might be able to nick some old fruit Billy had on his cart. He's taken it all off and put it in crates to fix the wheel.'

'How is your friend?' She adjusted her shawl as it had slipped from her shoulders and lifted her basket ready to make tracks.

Tommy shook his head sadly. 'Not so good, gal.' His eyes shone for a moment. 'I know I wasn't going to do this due to keeping a secret, but I'd like to take you to meet him later on, if you don't mind? As I trust you.'

She smiled. 'No, I don't mind at all,' she said.

'Come on then,' he said with a gleam in his eyes.

He took her by the hand to cross the busy road, leading her down the alleyway through the rabbit warren of lanes and passageways.

It would be good to be by the fireside for a warm and to see Tommy's ma once again and she wondered what Billy was like.

Chapter Eight

Billy was busy inspecting the wheel from his cart when they arrived. He was holding the cartwheel up against the light from a pale wintery sun. He turned and smiled at them as he noticed their approach. He was a handsome young man, Angeline thought. His hair was dark and curly and his eyes almost black. Around his neck, he sported a red and white spotted neckerchief, just above his long leather waistcoat which he wore over a thick brushed woollen shirt. His trousers were thick ribbed corduroy which had obviously seen better days but were his working gear.

'How's it going with that?' Tommy asked as he drew up near.

'One of the wooden spokes dislodged when I rolled the cart over some deep ruts in the road this morning. I've managed to fix it and should be able to get the wheel back on in time for this afternoon's trade,' he said cheerfully. Then his eyes fixed on Angeline. 'And who is this?' He smiled warmly. 'Aren't you going to introduce us?'

'This here is Miss Angeline Barker from Bow!' Tommy said with a theatrical gesture of the hand as though he were introducing a famous stage actress.

Angeline brought her hand to her mouth to stifle a giggle.

'Pleased to meet you, Miss Angeline Barker from Bow!' greeted Billy as he grinned broadly.

Angeline dropped her hand to her side as she smiled at him. 'Likewise.'

'Has Ma got anything on the go in there?' asked Tommy.

'You and your stomach, our kid. Yes, she's made some currant buns, go and have one each and then when I've finished sanding this wheel you can help me get it back on again!'

Tommy nodded eagerly. 'Come on, Angel,' he said patting her on the back, 'let's get inside in the warm.'

Angeline didn't need asking twice and that was the first time Tommy had referred to her as "Angel". It was a name only used occasionally for her by family members and those she was close to, so she liked it a lot as it was used less frequently these days.

***

Mrs Featherstone was seated in the corner of the room at a treadle sewing machine when they arrived, head down, deep in concentration as she fed some material through it. The whirring of the machine and the attention she was paying to her work caused her to miss the pair's entrance. Angeline hadn't noticed a sewing machine there when she'd last paid a visit and she looked at

Tommy in puzzlement with her head tilted on one side.

'Our Billy bought it for Ma off a customer the other day. She used to work as a seamstress, see, when she was young.'

Angeline nodded.

Tommy's mother looked up as they approached. 'Hello, you two,' she greeted with a smile. 'I'll just finish off this seam and then I'll be with you. I daresay you'd like a currant bun each?'

'Yes, please Mrs Featherstone. Shall I put the kettle on for you?' Angeline offered.

'There's a good girl you are, I could do with a cuppa myself. Fill it from the pump outside. The kettle's near the hearth, there's not enough left inside it.'

'I'll show you where the pump is.' Tommy took her basket from her and placed it on the table and then he lifted the old black, soot-caked kettle and escorted her up the cellar steps and over to the pump which was in the middle of the yard surrounded by houses. 'I expect you know how to use it, love?'

She nodded. 'Yes, there's one like this near where I live. You go and help your brother with that wheel if you like and I'll get the tea underway.'

'All right then, if you're sure?'

'Yes. Go on.' She glanced across at Billy who appeared to be sizing the wheel up as though it were ready to attach to the cart. The timing couldn't have been better.

Once the wheel was secured Billy was on his way, to sell his fruit and veg around the streets in the area which included Shoreditch and Bethnal Green. Tommy returned to the living room just as Angeline brought a tray of tea and currant buns into the room.

Mrs Featherstone stood and moved away from her sewing machine. 'Well, that's me done. I need a break,' she smiled at the pair of them. 'Been working on that frock all morning.'

'Aye, Ma's been up since the crack of dawn to finish it.' Tommy explained.

As she drew near, Angeline looked up at her. 'What sort of frock is it?'

'A posh one!' laughed the woman. 'It's for a lady from one of those big houses. I used to make them for her years ago when I worked in a fashion store on the high street. I hadn't worked as a dressmaker for years but one day, I ran into her when I was out shopping and she asked if I still worked at Hardimans. That was the store, you see. I explained that someone new had taken it over and their standards had slipped. It was then she asked me if I was still a dressmaker as she'd be very interested. She'd admired my work back then, the attention to detail. She said I should think about working from home and cut out the middleman. She also said she could get me some customers. So it got me thinking, and then when our Billy had the chance to purchase this one second-hand, I almost fainted. Me, a dressmaker again, after all these years.'

Angeline noticed a twinkle in the woman's eyes as she spoke. Dressmaking was obviously something she was passionate about, though in her opinion she'd do well to sell her cakes too as they were totally scrumptious.

The woman took a seat at the table and Angeline stood to pour the tea for them all. When she had done so, Mrs Featherstone looked at her. 'Go over and see it if you like, tell me what you think.'

Angeline nodded eagerly and she went over to the corner where the dress was draped over the side of the wooden table the machine was set in to.

'Don't be shy. Pick it up!' urged Mrs Featherstone. 'Your hands are clean, aren't they?'

Angeline inspected them thoroughly and nodded with a smile and then she lifted the dress. Prisms of light hit it from a small window above her head from which could be seen the feet of people passing by. She was in absolute awe of the woman's craftsmanship. The dress material was a lilac moiré taffeta and the workmanship that was going into it was evident. It had puffed sleeves and frilled ruffles on the bodice, nipped in by a tiny waist.

'It's beautiful,' gasped Angeline, as Mrs Featherstone nodded and smiled as if pleased with her own work.

'Thank you, darlin'.'

'But how did you afford all the materials to make it? If you don't mind me asking.'

'Oh, that's easy, I asked Mrs Monroe for half the money now and half when it's completed. I know the best places to get these things, the rolls of material, the required haberdashery etc. The lady trusts me as I've worked on gowns for herself and her daughters before now. This one is for her eldest daughter, Adelaide. She turns twenty-one next month and there's to be a grand ball at the house. I think her mother's hoping it will all lead to a new suitor for her daughter.'

Angeline thought it marvellous that Mrs Featherstone's handiwork could have a hand in some young woman's romance. She replaced the dress as she found it and took her cup of tea and Tommy's from the tray, handed his to him and took hers to sit near the hearth. 'But I was thinking, Mrs Featherstone...' she said softly, hoping she didn't overstep the mark or be intrusive towards the woman's business. 'But your cakes are so good, you could sell those too!'

'Oh, I used to but demand got so large that I couldn't cope with it all on my own.' She put her index finger to her chin as she gazed thoughtfully at Angeline, 'but I suppose if I had a helper, I could start it up again.'

'Now that's an offer for you,' Tommy grinned at Angeline.

'Oh, any time, Mrs Featherstone. I'm always up for making money to help the family. What would I have to do?'

'Deliveries mostly around the neighbourhood

and helping me in the kitchen. It would have to be a part-time thing for me though as the dress-making takes up a lot of my time.'

'Well, that's an offer you mustn't refuse!' Tommy took a bite out of his currant bun.

'Let me know then, Mrs Featherstone. I'd like to help you out if I may. I work mainly in the mornings selling my matches and there's a little lunchtime trade, but I should be free most afternoons to help for time being.'

'I'll let you know, dear. I can always send a message with my Thomas.'

Tommy's mouth was so stuffed full of currant bun that he couldn't reply, he just made a guffawing sound, gesturing with a head nod. He swallowed, and looking at his mother said, 'Any more buns, Ma? This is *so* good.'

Angeline was just about to chastise him for making his mother go off to the scullery to get more when she realised there was method in his madness. He wanted more to feed his friend Bobby. Now she was going to have to pretend she'd eaten hers as well. So taking a final bite, she slipped the remainder into her skirt pocket.

Ma returned shortly with the plate, on top of which there were five glazed buns. 'Now then, I have to keep one each for the rest of the lads but you may have another, Thomas. Oh, and Angeline, you must have been hungry! For one so small you have a terrific appetite.'

'Yes, Ma, she eats like a horse!' He winked

mischievously at Angeline.

If it wasn't that these buns were going to a very good cause she'd have clocked him one.

***

As they left the property with both currant buns wrapped in her neckerchief for his friend, safely hidden in her basket, Tommy glanced hesitantly in Angeline's direction.

'What is it?'

'I need to get some more clobber for Bobby,' he said solemnly. 'That place I've got him hidden in is very damp, he's developed a bit of a cough. Could do with getting him some more blankets and all.'

Angeline had every sympathy for the lad after what she'd seen her own mother go through with her chest. The racking, harsh bouts of coughing and her feeling cold most of the time. Her heart went out to the lad, even though she'd not met him yet.

'He could do with some building up by the sound of it.' She bit on her bottom lip as she deliberated. 'I don't think a couple of buns will help him all that much if that place is as damp as you say it is. Especially not this time of the year, Tommy.'

Tommy shook his head sadly as they passed a couple of young children who were banging away on some old saucepans, making a right racket they were. Then their mother emerged from the house, and grabbing both by the arms, yanked them indoors. No doubt fed up with the noise.

Even those children as poor as they were, had it better than Bobby did right now.

Tommy led Angeline through several pathways past tumbledown-looking dwellings and then along a precariously placed plank of wood over some kind of stream until they reached what looked like an old warehouse that was three storeys high with lots of broken windows.

He sniffed loudly and wiped his runny nose on the back of his hand. 'Lots of folk won't venture here,' he whispered.

'Why's that?' Her forehead puckered up into a frown.

'Because it's teeming with rodents. Most are scared to venture here. Also, it's rumoured to be haunted.'

A shiver coursed Angeline's spine. 'How come?'

'The boss of this place, it was some kind of cotton mill in the old days, was a right mean so and so and a bit of a tyrant to the workers. He made Ebenezer Scrooge seem a very kind and generous fellow, if you get my drift?' She nodded at him. 'Anyhow, he died and all his workers threw a big party here when he'd gone. There was singing and dancing and a bit of the hard stuff going on.'

'Hard stuff?' she wrinkled her nose.

'Aye, spirits and that sort of thing. Rum and Whisky. So they got very drunk between them all, that glad they were that he passed but then it's rumoured that the culprits who arranged the joyful jamboree, died, one by one in mysterious circumstances.'

'How?'

'Well, one fell into the machinery, another hung himself, another drowned in a large vat outside the building...It was said it was the ghost of the old boss come back to haunt them all!'

Angeline held the open palm of her hand to her chest. 'How dreadful.' She exhaled loudly. 'That story gives me the shivers...'

He shot her a wicked smile and she couldn't make out whether he was making it up to frighten her or not.

They entered the building through a ramshackle wooden door, hanging off its hinges, and from above, Angeline could hear rhythmic drips of water coming from somewhere. This place was so large and echoing it gave her the creeps. She wanted to yell to him to get out of there but she realised they must check on Bobby's welfare.

'Come on,' urged Tommy, he's usually on the ground floor at the back of the building. I told him to stay down here as it's unsafe above, those floorboards are rotting away.

'It's freezing in here.' Angeline's teeth chattered and she was shocked that it was even colder than she'd expected, all the while wondering how on earth anyone could survive a night, never mind several in this place.'

'Be careful by here,' Tommy warned, 'there's a plank we need to walk across to get to the back of the building. Watch you don't slip off it as it gets a bit slippery when it's wet as there's green slimy stuff growing on it.'

She nodded at him. 'When did you see Bobby last?'

'The day before yesterday, he weren't too good then to tell you the truth. I was all for making him come with me and beggar his uncle, but he begged me to let him stay here, he's that petrified of the man.'

'He must be to prefer to stay in here.'

Further still until finally, they reached the back of the building and a door that was shut. 'Bobby, it's only me and a friend of mine called, Angeline!' Tommy cried out.

There was no reply forthcoming. Tommy tried the door knob but it wouldn't budge. He turned to look at Angeline with a look of wide-eyed dread on his face. 'He might have bolted it from the inside.'

He tried banging on the door with one fist and then the other, two at a time. 'He might have passed out,' he said.

Angeline laid down her basket and banged on the door with her fists as well, but there was no reply.

'Come on,' she urged. 'Let's put our shoulders into this and try to force the door open by pushing on the bolt.' She'd seen Michael do that once when Sammy had got himself locked in the privy.

Both did the best they could but it wouldn't budge. Finally, Tommy said, 'I think I need to get one of my brothers to help.'

Angeline noticed that Tommy's bottom lip was trembling now and she just knew he feared Bobby was dead.

'Yes, there's nothing else you can do. We can't leave him here, you'll just have to risk telling your brother.'

He nodded. 'Billy should be around this area somewhere on his cart, I'll go and see if I can find him and bring him back here but if I can't...' he chewed his lower lip.

'If you can't, you are just going to have to fetch someone else to help. You can't risk him being locked in there any longer in this weather.' Angeline shook her head. She felt for the lad and Tommy too.

'You stay here then, in case he does answer and you can tell him I've gone for help.'

Angeline gulped, she didn't much feel like staying in this horrible, echoing building but realised she had to. 'All right.' She nodded her agreement at him. 'Go now as quick as you can.'

It seemed an age as she waited for him to return with help. 'Bobby,' she said softly through the door. 'Tommy, your mate, has gone to get help. He's going to get you out of there. I'm his mate too, my name's Angeline Barker...'

She couldn't be sure, but she thought she heard a faint moan, so decided to carry on talking to him saying anything to try to keep him awake though she couldn't be sure he was conscious at all.

'I live near the Bow match factory. You know of

it I'm sure. It's got a big chimney stack on top and makes a loud noise with the hooter. I live with my older brother Michael and my sister Eliza, they're both older than me. I also have a younger brother and sister and...'

There was that noise again. A groan this time. Louder.

'If you can hear me, Bobby, will you please knock on the door to let me know? I think you're too weak to talk right now. There it was, a light rap on the door. Her heart soared. He was alive, he really was alive.

'I heard that Bobby. Now keep your strength up and rest until help comes and we're going to get you out of there and into a warm bed.' She had no idea if that's what would happen in reality but she had to keep the lad's spirits up, and most importantly of all, she realised she needed to keep him conscious.

An uncle of hers had once fallen from a ladder, hitting his head and was out spark cold for a few minutes, when he came to, she remembered someone in attendance saying it was best to keep him awake in case he lapsed into a coma. So that's what she figured was the best thing to do here. She kept on talking to Bobby, telling him all manner of things about her family though not that her father had left them all nor that he was a chimney sweep like the boy's uncle was. That might be enough to terrify the lad. So she told him all about the angel doll and that it might be worth something, then she told him about Michael's job on the market and how fit he was hefting around heavy carcasses.

Then finally, she heard voices and there was Tommy with Billy in tow behind him. She heaved a sigh of relief as they approached. 'He's still alive in there,' she said.

'How do you know that?' Tommy's eyes widened.

'I've heard him groan and I told him to knock on the door which he did. I didn't keep him knocking though as I think he doesn't have the strength so I just kept talking to him and telling him help was on the way.'

Billy's expression looked grave but he nodded at her. 'Good girl. Now then I've got a crowbar with me, so keep out of the way both of you.'

The pair moved back and Tommy whispered, 'He keeps that with him in case he gets attacked on his round.'

'Just as well,'

It wasn't a moment before Billy was shouting to Bobby. 'Try to keep well clear of the door, lad. I'm going to break it open for you.'

There was no sound from inside, but all realised it had to be done whether Bobby was behind the door or not. His life needed saving.

Billy wedged the crowbar in the side of the door, leveraging it hard back and forth several times over. Finally, there was the sound of splitting wood, and carefully he pried the door open and flung the crowbar to one side.

'All right, lad. I've got you,' he said, as he entered the room, stooping, he scooped the lad up into his strong arms.

Both children watched as Billy carried Bobby out of there as though he were a rag doll as he gently cradled his fragile form. 'Tommy, get me crowbar and carry it to the cart. Both of you come with me now. This place is too dangerous for anyone to be in here. It's only fit for the rats.'

Tommy retrieved the crowbar and Angeline lifted her basket from the floor and they followed Billy to the awaiting cart outside.

Chapter Nine

When they arrived at the cart in the lane just across from the building, Angeline watched as Billy slipped a silver coin into a young lad's grubby palm. He'd obviously asked him to keep an eye on it as it was still carrying a lot of produce. Thankfully, the lad had been honest as he could have made off with a lot of it and tried to sell it for himself. Especially the sacks of potatoes and carrots.

'You two best make your own way home as I'll be quicker without you. It's too much strain for the donkey to take us all back there.'

'But where will you take him?' Tommy asked, fearful now in case the boy's uncle should get wind of this.

'Don't fret none, our kid. I'll take him to our house and Mam can try to get some soup down him. Might have to call the doctor out with that terrible wheezy chest he has there.' Billy had settled Bobby on the back of the cart under some old empty hessian sacking to keep him warm.

'We'll follow you over!' Tommy shouted to his brother and waved. 'And thank you, Billy!'

The pair watched as he drove the cart away over the rickety cobbles and all the while, Angeline thought what a blessing it was that the cartwheel had been mended today and mainly that they'd got to Bobby in time.

***

Tommy sauntered along quietly with his head down as they headed home. Angeline didn't like to see him like that so she tried to keep his spirits up. 'Well anyway, Bobby will be safe and warm now,' she said cheerfully. 'You couldn't have done any more.'

He stopped walking for a moment and turned to face her and she noticed a tear cutting a path down his grubby-looking cheek.

'Don't you see?' he sniffed, 'It's me what got Bobby into this trouble in the first place? Me and my daft idea to hide him away. I should have made him come back home with me and beggar his uncle.'

'It's easy to say that now but at the time your intentions were good, Tommy...' she reached out and touched his arm in a mark of reassurance.

He swallowed hard and nodded. 'Well yes, my intentions were good but what I did was wrong.'

She could tell that nothing she said was going to make the slightest bit of difference until he knew his friend was going to be all right, so she accompanied him in silence back to his home. The cart was parked outside the cellar steps and Billy was unloading the produce to take indoors for the time being.

He looked at them both with an urgency in his

eyes. 'I'm getting shot of this lot so I can go and fetch the doctor for the boy.'

Tommy looked at him with such sad doleful eyes that Angeline's heart went out to him. 'Will he be all right do you think?'

Billy shrugged. 'It's hard to say. But what do you think you were playing at keeping him in a place like that? You should have brought him home to Ma. She's got him by the fireside wrapped in a warm blanket and is feeding him some soup from a spoon. He's not said a word as yet.'

Angeline nudged Tommy so he might explain to his brother what this was all about but he said nothing, so she felt the need to defend him.

'He did it because the lad's uncle, who is a chimney sweep, has been cruel to him. Making him climb chimneys, sticking pins in his bare feet to force him up them. And once he got trapped and thought he'd never get out. He's also been beating him. Can't you imagine how scary that must have all been? Tommy's only been trying to help him.'

'Oh?' said Billy. Now looking remorseful for his harsh words to his brother. 'You meant well then. Let's not look on the black side, eh? Let's get the doctor over to check on the little guy's health and then we'll think about what to do about the situation.'

Tommy forced a smile, but Angeline could tell he felt dreadful.

'I'm going to have to go back home now,' she said softly. 'Hope all will be well. I'll see you tomorrow, maybe?' She made eye contact with him.

He just stared at her, his eyes brimming with tears and she guessed he didn't want to break down in front of her, so she just nodded at Billy who returned the nod, and she turned to walk the fair distance home alone.

***

When Angeline returned home it was now almost two o'clock and she opened the door to the property expecting to hear Eliza call out to her but all was quiet. Her eyes scanned the living room, there wasn't even a fire lit and to her dismay, the cardboard, glue and string were still on the table where she'd left them for her sister that morning.

Gritting her teeth with anger, she climbed the stairs. Maybe Eliza was in their bedroom prettying herself up for George? But no, it was as it had been left that morning with the beds neatly made up.

'Angeline!' Ma's weak voice cried out.

Her heart slumped, in her anger she'd forgotten all about Ma and her needs. Pasting a cheerful-looking smile on her face, she made her way to her room to see her mother sitting up in bed holding her chest as she coughed.

'Can you fetch a nip for me please, darlin'?'

A nip for Ma meant only one thing—she was craving her brandy again and she'd done so well too going without it lately.

Angeline's forehead wrinkled into a frown. 'I don't know if brandy will be all that good for you, Ma. You need to see a doctor really.'

'Oh, we ain't got the money for that.'

'Well, when we do, that's the first thing that's needed. Meanwhile, there's some cough mixture left downstairs, I'll fetch you that and a cup of tea. Have you eaten?'

Ma shook her head. 'Not since that porridge you made me first thing this morning.'

Angeline sighed softly. 'Then I'll fetch you something to eat too. What happened to Eliza? She was supposed to have made up those matchboxes by now!'

'She said she was popping out for an hour so I didn't worry too much.'

'What time was that?'

'Not long after you'd left this morning.'

Angeline shook her head all the while thinking, *I'll flamin' kill her! I asked her to do one thing! One thing that's all to help us out and now she's wasted the money I spent buying all that stuff yesterday!*

As if Ma could sense what she was thinking, she smiled and said, 'Maybe I could help?'

'No, Ma,' Angeline said firmly. 'Eliza was supposed to do it. I'll make you that tea and fetch that medicine, then I'll make a start on the matchboxes until she gets home.'

She approached her mother and touching her crepe-like hand said, 'You can help when you feel a bit better.'

Ma smiled at her and closed her eyes. She guessed she'd be asleep by the time she got downstairs. This was so unfair.

Angeline removed her shawl and hung it on the peg on the back of the door. Then she set about lighting the fire, which was already laid by her that morning. And then she poured water into the kettle from a jug she'd filled from the pump earlier. She was glad she'd done so as she didn't much feel like a trek out there after the morning she'd had. Soon a blazing fire was underway and the kettle was placed on it to boil.

She went to fetch the medicine bottle from the larder and was dismayed to see there wasn't all that much left of the dark brown syrupy concoction. Ma swore it worked wonders but Angeline doubted it did a lot of good. For all she knew, it might be sugared water as her mother had bought it a couple of weeks back from a door-to-door salesman who was probably no better than some sort of carnival quack who sold "cure-alls" from the back of his horse-drawn caravan.

Puffs of steam from the hearth alerted Angeline to the kettle boiling merrily away. She made a pot of tea then she used the remainder to fill the stone hot water bottle for Ma. She'd warm her up in bed first with a cup of tea and a couple of spoonfuls of medicine, then later she could come down by the fireside for a bowl of nourishing soup. There was some leftover in the pan from yesterday after Michael had brought home a large hambone with a little bit of meat left on it which she'd used in the soup with some potatoes and onion.

After settling her mother upstairs, Angeline

removed her mud-caked boots and sat by the fireside, staring into the orange flames thinking of all sorts: Eliza's laziness, her father's selfishness, Tommy, and how upset he was today and most of all, poor Bobby. The lad had looked like a bag of bones when Billy lifted his skeletal body onto the cart.

How were they all going to manage? They could do with some luck.

And then there was a sharp knock on the door.

Warily, she laid down her teacup and went to answer, first looking through the side window to ensure it wasn't her father there, but she relaxed when she saw it was Mr Goodman. Some news about the doll at last!

Chapter Ten

Angeline drew open the door and saw the man had the doll all boxed up in his hands and he was offering it to her so she took it.

'I'm sorry to have to tell you this,' he began before she even had a chance to greet him, 'but the doll isn't as I thought it might be...'

She tilted her head to one side, puzzled. 'How'd you mean, Mr Goodman? Would you like to come inside for a moment?'

'No, no, thank you. I've left my assistant taking care of the shop and I don't like to leave him too long in case we get any awkward customers, you see.'

She nodded.

'The doll is a forgery, I'm afraid, that's why I'm returning it to you. A good copy at best so it's not really worth all that much.'

'B...but I can't afford to pay you back for pawning it,' she protested.

He smiled at her now. 'And you don't have to. I decided as you've been through a lot over Christmas and I'm disappointing you, that you shall have it back as a gift from me to you. I don't want any money. I reckon you should keep it and enjoy it like my friend's wife does with her collection of dolls. Something pretty to look at. Who knows, someday you might be able to afford the real thing!'

She seriously doubted that but didn't say so, just smiled at the man. 'Thank you so much, Mr Goodman.'

He nodded and went on his way and she closed the door behind him. It was turning out to be an eventful day, to say the least.

***

It was late that evening before Eliza made an appearance, breezing in through the door with her hair covered in snowflakes, brushing them down and removing her shawl, shaking it out and hanging it on the peg on the back of the door, she turned to face Angeline.

There was a glint in her brown eyes and a smile plastered all over her face.

Angeline folded her arms and tapped her foot angrily. 'And where were you today?' She asked. 'I've been standing out in the cold selling matches while you ought to have assembled those matchboxes! Then I came home to find Ma in bed with no food inside her.' This was getting too much to bear.

'Please forgive me, Angeline, this hasn't been a normal day. It weren't that I didn't want to help it's just that George had something to give to me, a surprise that couldn't wait!'

Angeline blinked. Whatever it was had put the

biggest smile on her sister's face and she hadn't seen her so happy in ages. It was hard to continue being angry with her as she danced around the table, much to the delight of Sammy and Joanna who both sat there tucking into their bowls of soup and crusty bread. They both laid their spoons down, their hunger forgotten in the melee.

'Well, aren't you going to tell us?' Angeline stared hard at her sister for some sort of explanation.

Eliza said, 'Quick kids, lift yer bowls of soup and plates of bread!'

Both children exchanged amused glances with one another as their sister whipped away the white lace tablecloth and put it over her head as she sang, 'Here comes the bride, here comes the bride, tra la la la tra la la de de la!' to the sounds of *Wagner's Bridal Chorus*.

Angeline frowned with confusion. Surely not?

'Ain't yer pleased for me?' said Eliza still standing there with the lace cloth on her head.

'Pleased about what?'

'George has got a job working on the docks and he's asked me to marry him!' She exclaimed as if it was the best thing in the world.

'But you're so young!' Angeline stuck out her bottom lip in disbelief at what she was hearing.

'I am not. I'm fifteen now but I shall be sixteen soon enough. In any case, I could have wed before now if I'd wanted to!'

'You're forgetting one thing, Eliza!'

'Oh yeah, what's that?' Eliza's eyes were flashing with indignation now.

'You need Pa's consent to marry as you're under the age of twenty-one!'

Eliza's face immediately creased as her smile disappeared and now Angeline felt awful for popping her sister's bubble of joy.

'I suppose you could ask him though, you were always his favourite.'

Eliza smiled again. 'You know what, you're right. I can wrap him around my little finger if I want to.'

The problem Angeline realised was that with Pa his permission would surely come at a cost and once he realised his future son-in-law was going to work on the docks and earn a living wage, then he might want to keep them sweet to see what he could get from the pair of them. But she kept her thoughts to herself.

'When did he ask you to marry him then?'

'Just this morning he called here on his way back from speaking to the foreman at the docks who has assured him of regular work. I was just about to start assembling those blessed matchboxes when there was a knock on the door. Oh, it was ever so romantic. Ma was still upstairs and everyone else had left the house, so there was just the two of us. For the time being he's bought me a little "engagement ring" from the dolly shop. I know it's not the real thing but it will do for now. It's just brass with a little pasted glass but it could pass muster for a real engagement ring.' She flashed it beneath her sister's nose.

Angeline had to admit that it did look real enough, though she guessed it might not be too long before the glass "diamond" fell out of its setting.

'Yes, it's really lovely and good luck to you both,' she said, hugging her sister warmly towards her.

As they drew apart, Angeline said, 'Mr Goodman called when you were out. It's bad news about the doll.'

'Oh?'

'It's a fake, a forgery of the real thing, so has little value.'

'Oh, I am sorry to hear that.' Eliza rubbed her sister's shoulder in sympathy.

'One good thing though,' said Angeline brightening up, 'he's given it back to me and I don't have to pay him a thing. So I'm going to keep it as the gift that it was intended for me.'

'Well that's good news at least,' said Eliza removing her impromptu veil from her head, folding it and replacing it on the table. Meanwhile, Sammy and Joanna had been unimpressed with their sister's wedding news and had finished off their bread and soup and now gone upstairs to play. She paused for a moment before deliberating. 'Look, I am sorry about today. I've let you down. I promise I'll make it up to you and make a start with those matchboxes tonight.'

Angeline beamed. 'Well if you do, I'll help you

this once.'

'That's decided then. I'll just change into something more suitable and make a start.'

It was then Angeline realised her sister had been wearing her Sunday best dress beneath her shawl. Only noticeable when she saw her hang the shawl on the door peg. Had she been expecting today's proposal from George?

'Shall I fix you something to eat first?'

Eliza shook her vibrant curls. 'I've already eaten, thank you. George took me to the pie shop to celebrate. I won't be a tick. I'll call in on Ma when I go upstairs to change out of my best dress.'

Angeline smiled. It seemed as if today was partly expected then with Eliza being dressed up and George having the money to splash out on a meal at the pie shop. Why on earth hadn't she explained she couldn't assemble those boxes earlier today? Didn't make any sense to her.

The main thing though was now Eliza was happy and on board to help out on this money-making venture. All hands on deck were needed right now.

***

It was pitch black outside when Angeline rose from her bed the following morning. She hadn't had much sleep as she'd been up until half past two that morning helping her sister assemble those matchboxes and the sweater would be calling for them soon. By rights it ought to be Eliza rising to pass them on to him but being the kind sort she was after Eliza's good news yesterday, she figured she'd give her sister a bit of a lie-in but with a warning she was on her own now making up those boxes. Sammy and Joanna were allowed to help for only one hour each after school, she didn't want it to affect their work thereby burdening them with taking on long hours to help out at home.

She hadn't seen much of Michael lately as he'd been working overtime at the butcher shop trying to grasp every extra penny he could. She wondered if he knew about Eliza's wedding proposal yet. She guessed not.

Eliza had decided she was going to try to find their father and seek his permission for a wedding to go ahead. He shouldn't be too difficult to locate as he was either with that floozie barmaid or propping up a bar in one of several pubs or taverns in the town.

Angeline poured some water from the jug into the large matching porcelain bowl and quickly washed her face and hands, a cat's lick her mother would have called it as that's what it amounted to but it was far too cold to stand on ceremony this morning. Then she dressed herself in her working clothes: a worsted skirt and thick cotton blouse, thick woollen stockings and boots. No time for one hundred strokes of her hair with the hairbrush this morning, she just ran the brush through it several times, easing out any knots and tied it up with a ribbon.

Downstairs, she stoked up the fire with a metal

poker. Michael must have only just left the house as she touched the teapot on the table and it was still warm, though not hot enough to drink. Sighing, she realised the kettle was half empty, so she'd need to fill it up from the pump outside.

Thankfully, it wasn't frozen over, so she was able to leverage the rusted iron rod up and down several times to get enough water for tea for them all.

She returned to the house and poured the water into the kettle from the wooden pail, then set it to boil on the fire, which was now blazing merrily away. As she stared into its orange, yellow and red flames, she wondered what today might have in store for her.

***

The rancid smell caused Angeline to gag as she made her way through the narrow squalid streets towards Tommy's home. For some reason today the odour was worse than usual. Her Ma had told her that it wasn't so long ago that there'd been an outbreak of cholera before Angeline had been born. It was thought to have been caused by London's growing population, where there was overcrowding in some areas like Whitechapel and beyond. It was said to be a waterborne disease caused by filthy sanitation. She hoped that wasn't going to happen again as according to Ma, the disease had wiped out a lot of folk.

Angeline had been out selling her matches at the same pitch that morning and Tommy hadn't shown up to help her like he'd promised he would. Standing on that corner, with her nerves on edge in case Pa showed up and shook her until her teeth rattled, wasn't much fun for her. If this was going to continue, she'd need to return to her usual pitch outside the Sampsons shop back home, but trade was better in Tommy's neck of the woods.

As she made her way towards the cellars, she wrapped her shawl tightly around her, there was a chill wind this morning which made her think that maybe snow was on the way again. Thankfully, the pavements and side paths were clear of the stuff at the moment.

Why hadn't Tommy turned up today, though?

As she approached the property, she was about to find out why.

Billy was standing outside with another, taller young man, who had similar features and they were both trying to get rid of someone.

'I want to see me nephew right now!' The man was yelling at them while jabbing his index finger in their faces. 'This is sacrilege. He's me flesh and blood, all I have left of me sister, Rose.'

Anyone passing might have thought it a pitiful tale but then a shiver coursed Angeline's spine as she realised it must be Bobby's uncle. One all-over glance of the man could tell her that, his soot-caked clothing and then affirmation from a pile of sweep's brushes that were stacked against the wall. The man's face was so grimy that the whites of his eyes stood out as he spoke.

'And I'm telling you,' said Billy fiercely, 'that you have no right to that boy at all. He's petrified of you and because of you, he might well have died.'

'No,' said the boy's uncle, 'he was still fit and well when he was in my charge. I want to know what's been going on as I was told the lad is now sick.'

Angeline, who up until now was the unseen observer, frowned. How did the man know something had happened to Bobby and where he was? Didn't make any sense to her.

'Now, I'm taking him away from here and we'll say no more about it,' said the uncle, as he made to make his way down the cellar steps only to be yanked away from them by the other man who by now she assumed was another of Tommy's brothers.

'Over our dead bodies!' yelled Billy.

'Well if that's your final word,' said the uncle, collecting his brushes from the wall, 'then I shall have to report to the old bill that a kidnap has taken place. For that's what it amounts to.'

'Aye, go ahead,' shouted the other brother, 'and we'll tell the police that you forced the young lad up chimneys when it's no longer legal to do so. Now put that in your pipe or should I say chimney and smoke it!'

Bobby's uncle scowled and made off with his brushes bypassing her as he went as though she were invisible to him.

Then Billy turned and spotting her, said, 'Hello, love. Come to see our Tommy, have you?' He smiled.

She nodded. 'If it's a good time?'

'Yes, it is. Come inside. How long were you standing there for?'

'Long enough,' she shook her head. 'How does that man know where Bobby's staying?'

'Tommy, weren't it. He were that frightened that Bobby might die that he went looking for some medicine for him from an herbalist who just happened to have the local gossipmonger in attendance with her. Word got out and this is the result.'

She shrugged. 'He meant well though.'

Billy's eyes softened. 'Aye, he did. Oh,' he said turning towards his brother, 'you two won't have met. This is Miss Angeline Barker from Bow and this is me brother, Reggie.'

Both nodded at one another.

'Now come on then, I expect Ma's got the kettle on. Tommy is taking care of Bobby, trying to keep him cheerful and the like. But now word has got out where he is, I think he's going to have to move on soon.'

Angeline shook her head, sadly realising that there was no better place for the lad to be right now than with the Featherstone family but remaining where he was would put him in jeopardy.

***

The fire was crackling away merrily in the grate as they entered the room and Tommy glanced over to Bobby, who was reclining on the settee beside him with a thick blanket covering his slight form. The lad looked so much better than the previous day when he'd appeared so pale and limp. Now his cheeks were pink but of course, he still looked frail and his eyes seemed too large for his head.

'Hello, Angeline,' Tommy greeted as she approached. Then he glanced at her wicker basket of matches. 'Oh no,' he said shaking his head. 'I was supposed to be on the pitch with you this morning. I clean forgot as I was looking after Bobby then his uncle showed up, causing trouble.'

'Don't worry none, I know. I saw him outside.' Angeline smiled at the pair.

For a moment, Tommy seemed alarmed but then Reggie said, 'Don't worry, he came back a second time but we put him on his way though we think it's best Bobby move somewhere else for his safety now.'

Angeline noticed Bobby's bottom lip quivering. He'd obviously felt safe here with the family. What a shame that Tommy had let out more than he should about the lad to the herbalist. Couldn't be helped she supposed—that uncle of his seemed a determined sort anyhow and it might have happened at some time or another in any case.

Both older brothers made their way to the scullery in search of their mother as Angeline directed her gaze at Bobby.

'Hello,' she said softly. 'Are you feeling better today?'

The lad nodded at her. 'Thank you for everything, Angeline,' he said.

Blinking in astonishment she replied, 'Thank me for what? I haven't done anything, it was Tommy and Billy who helped you.'

He shook his head. 'But you kept me company by talking to me through the door. You gave me hope.' He began to cough into his hand.

'I'll fetch you some more medicine,' said Tommy, rising from the settee with some concern. It was obvious to Angeline how worried the lad was about his friend and how he might have made a bad situation even worse for the lad, even if his heart was in the right place at the time.

Bobby nodded.

'I'm glad I was able to help.' Angeline smiled at him, an idea beginning to form in her mind and she hoped it would work out.

***

'So these Sampsons who own a shop, they're a childless couple, are they?' asked Mrs Featherstone later when they were all taking tea together.

Angeline nodded. 'They're ever so kind.'

Both older brothers, their mother and Angeline, were seated at the table while Bobby and Tommy ate their slices of ginger cake and supped their tea on the settee.

Angeline swallowed a morsel of cake and took a sip of tea before answering. 'Now I can go there when I return home and ask if they're willing to take him in. They have plenty of room.' She knew that as Mrs Sampson had shown her into the upstairs of their living quarters once when she wanted to show her a new hat she'd bought for a wedding. She'd called her upstairs and shown her the three good-sized bedrooms.

Billy nodded. 'That sounds a grand idea to me. What do you think, Tommy?'

Tommy scowled. Of course, he wouldn't want to see his friend go elsewhere but when he turned to Bobby, the boy was smiling.

'Looks like Bobby thinks it a good idea, don't you, son?' said Reggie.

Bobby nodded enthusiastically. 'I love being here with you all and you've been so kind to me, every last one of you. But I no longer feel safe here now my uncle knows where I am.'

There was a murmur and she heard Billy whisper something to his mother. Then he averted his gaze in Angeline's direction. 'Can you talk with them as soon as you go back home?'

She nodded. 'Yes, I will do that,' she said with some determination.

Now all she hoped was that the couple would agree to her rather strange request out of the blue.

Chapter Eleven

Angeline stood deliberating outside the Sampson's shop. The nativity scene was still in the window as it was twelfth night tomorrow. She chastised herself for being so silly about being hesitant to just walk into the shop as she often did, but the reason for that she realised was because she felt guilty for what she'd intended to do with the angel doll she'd been gifted, even though it was hers to do with as she wished. But now, she tried to reassure herself that she had done no wrong as she was trying to help her family. In any case, she still had the doll at home and she was pleased about that as it was the most beautiful gift she'd ever been given.

The little bell above the door tinkled as she opened it, relieved to see there were no customers inside. Mr Sampson stood behind the wooden counter where he was writing something down in a hardbacked ledger book. He looked up at her over the rim of his glasses and smiled as she approached.

'Angeline, my dear!' he greeted, then he moved around from behind the counter to stand before her. 'How have you been, my child? We were so disappointed you didn't call over Christmas…'

Her heart slumped. She'd forgotten she'd promised his wife she would call. What must they think of her? Especially after receiving that beautiful gift from them. An ungrateful wretch, that's what.

As if sensing something was up, he studied her face with a look of concern in his eyes. 'What is it, Angeline? Has something happened?'

She swallowed as tears pricked the back of her eyes.

No, not now, please. I don't want to cry in front of Mr Sampson.

'Y…yes.' Her bottom lip trembled and to her horror, her shoulders racked with the upset of all that had occurred over the past couple of weeks.

'Hang on a moment there,' he said softly, 'I'll just fetch Margaret to attend to you in case anyone comes into the shop.'

She guessed it wasn't really about that at all, he just didn't know how to deal with a young girl breaking down in front of him as he'd never had a child of his own.

As her eyes glazed over, she took in her surroundings as she waited, the colourful glass jars of boiled sweets and the aromas of ham, cheese, pickles, oranges and other fruit that permeated her senses. It brought her some comfort, as did Mr and Mrs Sampson themselves. They were her rock to cling to as they were steady and stable, just what Bobby needed right now.

It wasn't a moment before Mrs Sampson was at her side and wrapping a comforting arm around her as she led her away into the back room.

'There, there,' she was saying in a whisper. 'You come and sit down by the fireside and tell me all about it.'

After removing her shawl and handing it to the woman, then settling down in the armchair as Mrs Sampson took the one facing her to listen, she drew in a shuddering breath and released it.

'Dad left us all on Christmas Eve to go off with a barmaid from The Kings Arms, not long after I'd been to see you that afternoon. So it's been really hard. Not only did he do that, but he took all the meat and poultry that our Michael had been given from Mr Styles, the butcher, to see us over the festive season. He probably sold it all in the pub.'

'How awful for you all,' said Mrs Sampson soberly as if she disapproved, though she did not voice her thoughts on that. 'You should have come to us, we'd have helped you all out, Angeline.'

Angeline smiled through her tears, knowing full well that really would have been the case.

'We managed in the end as my brother was able to get some offcuts of meat from Mr Styles and he's still earning a wage, and so do I with the matches, and even our Eliza is making matchboxes now to help out.'

'So, is that why we haven't seen you?' The woman sat forward in her armchair, her hands clasped together as she listened intently.

'Yes.' Angeline bit her lip as if it was only the partial truth. 'Anyhow, I found a busier pitch some distance from here where I can make more money selling matches and I met a young lad called Tommy...'

She went on to explain to the woman all about her new friend and his family and what had happened to Bobby as Mrs Sampson listened with great interest, awing and ahhing, every time Bobby's name was mentioned, even tearing up herself when she heard the final outcome and how the lad's uncle was now after him, probably to send him up chimneys again.

'That's dreadful, Angeline. So, he'll now stay with Mrs Featherstone and her family?'

'They think it's best that he now lives somewhere else out of his uncle's clutches but they don't know where best to send him.'

'I suppose he might be safer in the workhouse?'

'Oh no!' Angeline shook her head vigorously. No one had even mentioned that word to her until now and as realisation dawned, she figured that could well happen. She was going to have to come right out with it and ask the woman.

'But he would be safer in there, surely?'

'Please, Mrs Sampson. Would you take Bobby in here? He's a lovely lad. He won't eat much food and he could help you in the shop.'

Mrs Sampson's eyes widened as though the thought of taking in the young lad had not possibly occurred to her. 'Oh! I don't know if that's a good idea. Mr Sampson and myself, we're not getting any younger.'

'But you said so yourself that you'd always wanted a child and were sorry you hadn't been blessed with any children at all.'

'Yes, now I know I did. But that was when I was of childbearing age, I meant. Not now when I'm old enough to be the child's grandmother.'

'But you and Mr Sampson would make such great guardians for Bobby. It's here I always come when I need some kindness and someone to listen to me. I feel safe here.'

Mrs Sampson took in a deep breath and then she sighed. Then she glanced up at the ceiling as though mulling things over. 'Look, I won't make any promises as I'll have to speak to my husband first and discuss things in detail with him. I'll make him a nice meal tonight and let him rest after being on his feet all day, then I'll have an answer for you by this time tomorrow. How does that sound to you?'

In an instant, Angeline had shot out of her armchair, wrapped her arms around the woman's neck and rained kisses on her soft powdery cheek. The woman had the comforting scent of lavender on her person.

'Oh, Mrs Sampson, you won't regret this. You and Mr Sampson will make the most wonderful guardians.'

'Hold your horses!' chuckled Mrs Sampson. 'I still have to ask William yet.'

***

Much to Angeline's relief by the following afternoon, the Sampsons had decided they would allow Bobby to live with them, at least for the present as long as they weren't forced by law to return the lad to his kin.

Not only that, but Eliza had found their father who agreed that a marriage between her and George could go ahead.

At least some people were now happy but Angeline couldn't help feeling there was some sort of darkness lurking around the corner.

***

The first thing Angeline heard early next morning when it was still pitch black outside was Ma retching. Fearing the worst, that her lung illness had got the better of her, she rushed into Ma's bedroom to find her mother seated on the edge of the bed with a metal pail in front of her, heaving her heart out.

'What's the matter, Ma?' She asked, her voice full of concern.

Her mother lifted her head from the pail to look at her. 'It's nothing...' she said in a thin voice and then she laid down the pail and returning beneath the bedcovers, rested her head on the pillow.

'But it can't be nothing if you're feeling sick like that. Hang on, I'll fetch you a mug of water and a wet flannel. I'll be back soon.'

Ma nodded and closed her eyes.

Should she fetch the doctor to her? Angeline's

mind was a whirl of questions as she went to pour the water from a jug in the pantry. Thankfully there were plenty of receptacles filled with water this morning as Michael had gone out to the pump last night. She found a small bowl and filled that too with some water and laid a clean flannel inside of it.

When she returned upstairs, to her relief, her mother was sitting bolt upright in the bed, well propped up with pillows.

'Here, drink this,' she said offering the mug to her mother, who gratefully accepted and took a few sips.

She took the mug from her mother's hand and set it down on the bedside table, handing her the damp flannel which she'd just squeezed out. 'Here, give your face a wipe with this,' she said softly.

'Thank you. Whatever would I do without you, my girl? You really live up to your name, my precious Angel.'

Angeline smiled. It was a long time since her mother had referred to her by her pet name. 'How are you feeling now?'

'A lot better thanks.'

'Is it your chest again that's causing it? Coughing up phlegm and such?'

Her mother shook her head. 'No. It's…it's…'

'What is it?'

Ma's shoulders started to shake and then she began to cry.

'Aw, Ma. What's wrong?' She sat on her mother's

bed and wrapped a comforting arm around her fragile, thin body, allowing her to cry for a couple of minutes.

Then when the crying ceased, she looked up at her daughter and said, 'Angeline, I think I'm going to have a baby.'

Angeline's mouth opened and closed. A baby? It had been a few years since her mother was last pregnant and now she was in her forties. It would not be any good for her health in the current situation she now found herself in, that was for sure. The severe physical toll it would place on her fragile body sent a shiver down her spine.

'I don't know what to say, Ma. Had you planned on having another child?'

'No, no, no,' wept Ma. 'It's the last thing I need right now, another mouth to feed, another baby hanging off of me. Not with your father going off and abandoning us all like that. Whatever shall I do about it?'

Quite honestly, Angeline had not a clue. And she didn't know who to speak to about it either. Mrs Sampson might be her best bet for a sympathetic ear. But the woman would hardly be in a position to give any advice as she hadn't had any children of her own.

This was yet another mess that her father had helped to create.

***

A spring wedding was arranged for Eliza and George with the latter intending to pay for it all, while Pa claimed he'd contribute something but Angeline very much doubted it. Meanwhile, Ma was still suffering from the sickness, so one morning when it became particularly bad before she set off to head to her pitch at the Old Nichol area, she looked at her mother with concern, she was yet to rise from bed.

'Ma, don't you think you ought to see a doctor? Just to check you over.'

Ma raised her hand from beneath the bedcovers and waved an open palm at her. 'No. We need to save every penny we can.'

Angeline sat beside her on the bed and taking Ma's pallid hand, spoke softly to her. 'I've saved a bit of money. I'd like you to have it.' She pressed a silver shilling in her mother's hand.

'Look, we need you to keep that for food and the rent,' Ma said, groaning as another wave of nausea hit her. Her mother's complexion now a deathly shade of pale.

'Michael's got enough to pay the rent and fair play, Eliza has kept to her word with assembling those matchboxes. We can manage without it.'

Reluctantly, her mother took it from her. 'We'll see,' she said, and she laid back on the pillow and closed her eyes.

'I'll just drop Sammy and Joanna off at school, then I'll call around to see Doctor Montague, to see if he can call when I'm back home this afternoon,' she said firmly, not prepared to accept any ifs or buts.

Her mother appeared too exhausted to raise any further objection and seemed to be asleep by the time she'd closed the bedroom door. Angeline went downstairs where Eliza was busy pasting a matchbox together, with frown lines on her face as if deep in concentration, it was good to see.

'I'm just going to take the kids to school, Eliza.'

Sammy and Joanna, who had been sitting quietly on the settee, rose and stood near Angeline as though ready to leave the house.

'All right,' Eliza replied without even looking up from her task in hand.

'Just keep an eye on Ma, I'm going to try to get the doctor out later. Trust Pa to leave a late Christmas gift behind.'

Eliza nodded and lifting her head, looked at her sister. 'We mustn't be too hard on him though, he's given his blessing for the wedding to go ahead.'

Angeline exhaled a stifled breath. *I'll believe it when I see it!* She would never voice her concerns to Eliza as the girl tended to think the best of their father as she was his "blue-eyed girl", his absolute favourite, so she thought to say nothing for now.

'Ma's sleeping for time being. Make sure she takes her cough medicine mid-morning and then...'

'I know you tell me every day. Medicine mid-morning, followed by a cup of tea and a piece of toast because it's only then she feels able to eat something,' Eliza said, with a note of exasperation to her voice.

Angeline rolled her eyes, realising it was almost as though she, herself, had turned into a little mother. She knew she was too young to be in this position really but what choice did she have? Eliza wasn't exactly responsible. The only person she seemed responsible for was herself.

Sighing, she smiled at her younger brother and sister. They looked up to her for sure. Then she drew her shawl from the nail behind the door and wrapped it around her shoulders. Taking her wicker basket of matches over the crook of her arm, she turned to them.

'Come on you pair or you'll be late for school. Bye, Eliza. Don't forget what I said now.'

Eliza mumbled something unintelligible to her ears and then they were out of the door, Angeline feeling dismayed that it had started to snow again. It was not going to be the best day for standing on the street selling matches that was for sure.

***

Bertie Barker was having a nip of rum in the Kings Arms when a familiar face emerged through the double swing doors. Marching towards the bar as he stamped snow from his leather boots was, Arnold Swindler. Good grief. He hadn't seen the man in a long while. Last he'd heard he was working in the Shoreditch area cleaning chimneys with a young lad who he said was some sort of relation. Mind you, he shouldn't have been doing so. Bertie, himself, had long since stopped using climbing boys when the practice had been outlawed by Parliament.

It was Lord Shaftsbury who had succeeded in persuading Parliament to pass the "Chimney Sweepers Act of 1875". This ensured the annual licensing of chimney sweeps and the enforcement of the law by the police, finally preventing the employment of boys as chimney sweeps, though there were still some like Swindler who flouted the law and didn't much care either.

As Arnold Swindler turned from the bar to seek out a table, he spotted Bertie and raised a hand of greeting to him. Strange, the man wasn't smiling as he'd normally be whenever they ran into one another. What was wrong here?

'Come and join me, Arnold, me old mate,' Bertie beckoned.

The man nodded at him and made his way over to the copper-topped table and took a seat beside Bertie. It wasn't long before the barman followed and placed a jug of ale and a silver tankard down on the table.

Looking at the man, Arnold said, 'Could you fetch another tankard so my friend can join me in a drink?'

The barman smiled and made his way back to the bar, returning shortly with the extra tankard.

'What gives?' Bertie asked when the barman had departed.

Arnold glanced around the pub, it wasn't too busy so it was as if he feared being overheard. 'Got myself a bit of trouble, ain't I.'

'Oh, aye. What kind of trouble?'

'Some folks have taken against me and kidnapped me nephew.'

Bertie frowned. 'The climbing lad that you puts up the chimney?'

'Sssh!' said Arnold, waving his hand. He nodded his head. 'Yes.'

'But why would they do that?' Bertie took a long swig of ale and wiped the beery foam from his top lip with the sleeve of his jacket.

'They reckons it's 'cause I shouldn't be sending him up any chimneys.'

'Well, you shouldn't. I stopped taking on climbing lads a few years ago when it was outlawed.'

'But you never do much bloody work anyhow, Bertie. Laziest sweep I've ever known.' He winked at him and Bertie began to laugh, realising it was true.

'So, is there any way you can get him back with you?'

'Maybe if I have someone what can help me do it, I can.'

He dipped into his pocket and extracted a gold sovereign causing Bertie to gulp. 'Up for it?'

Bertie's eyes grew large and he began to salivate at the prospect of earning a sovereign.

'What would I need to do?'

Arnold leaned in towards his old mate and laid a hand on his shoulder. 'There'll be a bag of these for you if you bring my little Bobby back home. Now here's what you need to do...'

***

On her way home, Angeline called to Doctor Montague's house but his housekeeper said he was extremely busy that day as his partner in the practice was away at the moment and she'd be better off calling in the following morning.

Feeling disappointed, she made her way home and when she arrived on the main street that led to Christmas Alley, she noticed her father standing on the step of the pub in deep conversation with some man. There was something familiar about him, she felt she'd seen him before somewhere but couldn't quite place him as his face was slightly turned away. Not wanting to run into her father, she quickly darted down the alleyway and rushed inside the house, bolting the door behind her, panting heavily.

Taking time to catch her breath, she noticed it, the pile of cardboard still on the table. Her sister had only assembled a few matchboxes. Not again! This was getting to be a habit now. Once she might have forgiven, but twice!

She rushed upstairs to her mother's bedroom and nearly keeled over to find her bed was empty, the bedclothes thrown back in a heap. Where was she?

'Ma!' she cried out, running from room to room but all that came back to her was her own echoing voice. 'Ma! Where are you?'

Had her mother taken ill and maybe she

thought the worse of her sister as she hadn't put those matchboxes together when in fact, she'd had to take her somewhere as she was ill?

What should she do? The kids weren't due home from school for another hour and Michael was at work.

Then she heard it, the singing coming from outside in the yard. It was Ma's voice but it sounded slurred. Oh no! She was emerging from the privy swaying, holding a familiar bottle in her hand. She was drinking again. Why would she do that?

Because she's upset she's having another baby, that's why!

How did she manage to buy it? Then it occurred to her, that she'd given her mother a shilling before she'd left so they could pay for the doctor's visit later. Why hadn't she thought about keeping it safe and giving it to him in receipt of his visit when he could call later?

***

'Ma, what on earth are you doing out here in the perishing cold?' Angeline demanded as she took her mother by the arm and guided her back inside the house. She hadn't even had time to remove her shawl as yet, so she whipped it off her own shoulders and placed it around Ma's. Her mother wasn't even dressed properly. She still had a flannelette nightgown on and a thin bed jacket around her shoulders. If anyone took a glance at her feet they would have noticed the sodden carpet slippers on them. Ma's face looked flushed compared to the usual pasty colour and Angeline put that down to the bottle in her hand, only this time it wasn't a nip of brandy, it was a whole bottle of flamin' gin.

There appeared to be about a quarter of the bottle gone, so she immediately grabbed it from her mother's clutches and helped her with her free hand inside the house. 'We need to get something hot inside you,' Angeline said firmly. 'You must not drink that stuff as I've heard it might bring on a miscarriage in a pregnant woman.'

Oh no! It just occurred to her that maybe that's what her mother's intention had been. Gin wasn't her drink of choice. That's what all this was about. She hated the thought of carrying another child!

To her horror, her mother began to sob as Angeline staggered to get her indoors.

'That's better, Ma,' she said, closing the door behind them while trying to keep her voice on an even keel. It was no use shouting at her mother or losing her temper, it looked as if Ma was at her wit's end. She could swing for that sister of hers. If Eliza had been here where she ought to have been then this wouldn't have happened.

Angeline drew out a chair from the table and made her mother sit. 'I'm going to boil up the kettle and make you something. A hot toddy was out of the question as alcohol was the last thing Mam needed right now. Coffee would be good but they could never afford that, so she decided to make Ma a hot milky drink with a little sugar inside of it, then she was going to get her changed and back into bed.

She poured some milk from an earthenware jug into a small saucepan and placed it directly on the fire in the hearth. Then she turned for a moment to look at her frail and fragile mother who was now seated at the table with her head in her hands.

Drawing close to her and placing a hand of reassurance on her shoulder, softly she asked, 'Why did you do it, Ma? Why?'

Ma dropped her hands from her face and looked up at her daughter with glassy eyes. 'It weren't the craving for the alcohol, though now I've had a taste of it I want more. It was because I don't want this baby inside of me. It's part of *him*! That rotten scoundrel of a husband!' She began to sob again as she turned her face towards her daughter, and Angeline held her head close to her chest.

'Ma, we're all part of our father yet you love each one of us.'

Her mother drew away and sniffed. 'I know I do. Maybe I'm taking it out on the little wretch that ain't even formed inside of me yet. It's making me feel so ill. Far worse than I was on any of my pregnancies with you lot.'

Angeline guessed maybe it was because of her mother's age, now being that much older. 'Did you spend all of that shilling I gave you?'

Her mother shook her head. 'I have a tanner left.'

'Well return the sixpence to me. I'm going to put it towards getting the doctor out first thing tomorrow morning. His housekeeper said he's very busy today but if I call first thing I should be able to get him out.'

Ma nodded as though completely defeated by it all. And seeing her mother this way made Angeline feel defeated too but she was determined not to give up.

By the time she'd given her mother the hot milk and changed her into new night clothes and warm bed socks, she figured the best thing was to let her rest in bed.

She was just about to make a cup of tea for herself and take a rest when the door burst open and Eliza breezed into the living room, her hair and shoulders of her shawl covered in snowflakes. One brief glance at her sister told Eliza something was wrong.

'What's up?' her eyes widened.

'What's up!' Angeline gritted her teeth. 'I'll tell you what's up...you've abandoned what you were doing this morning to go off somewhere that you thought more important and you abandoned Ma too.'

'Oh, is that all you're concerned about? I've just returned, ain't I? I'll get those finished in time, especially with Sammy and Joanna's help,' she said, glancing at the cardboard and pot of glue on the table.

'It's not even so much about those ruddy

matchboxes! It's while you were out, Ma left here and bought herself a bottle of gin, still in her nightclothes!'

Eliza's jaw dropped. 'She what? But how did she get the money for gin anyhow?'

Now it was Angeline's turn to feel in the wrong. 'I gave her a shilling as I intended to fetch the doctor to her today, so I told her she could pay him with that.'

Eliza raised her eyebrows. 'He didn't show?'

Angeline shook her head. 'No. He's busy today, tomorrow there's more chance of a house call.'

'Well I am sorry, Angeline, but that weren't all my fault, was it? You shouldn't have given Ma that money.'

'I know that now but my intentions were good. Where were you anyhow?'

George called to see if I'd spoken to Pa and I told him I had and he's agreeable to our wedding. Then he asked to speak to him himself to ask for my hand in marriage. So I went with him to find Pa. As soon as I did, I left them together to talk and returned home hoping to catch up on my work. I had no idea Ma would have got up when I left. You know what she's like, often sleeping through the morning as she coughs so much at night.'

Angeline did know indeed. Her mother became exhausted after those bad bouts of coughing overnight. It was her usual routine to rest until midday most days so to be fair to her sister, she wasn't to know, though it would be foolish to leave

Ma unattended for too long.

There was a long silent pause between the pair until finally, Eliza bit her lip and looking at Angeline with remorseful eyes, said, 'I am sorry. I should have thought. It won't happen again, I just wanted to find Pa to sort all the wedding business out. George is old fashioned you see, he likes to do things properly and he wanted to ask Pa's permission man to man even though I'd already got it.'

Angeline smiled. 'Well, sounds like you've got a good 'un there—hang on to him.'

'I will, don't worry,' said Eliza, taking a seat at the table to get on with her work.

'I'll make us both a cup of tea,' Angeline said brightly, realising that she had a very forgiving nature. She had little choice as far as Eliza was concerned.

Chapter Twelve

Arnold Swindler had instructed Bertie on how to find Bobby; to do so he said, he must follow that young lad called, Tommy, he'd lead him to the boy. Arnold had been certain that the Featherstone family would have moved him on somewhere by now. Bertie had heard mention of the family name as they were well known in the area with their costermonger business, though he'd yet to encounter any of them.

Bertie stood outside the place where Arnold had told him the family lived. It looked even shabbier than the Barker Family residence. This area seemed to consist of various cellar-dwellings. He knew he had the right place as there was a wooden cart outside with the name "Featherstone Fruit and Vegetables" painted on it. No sign of a horse or donkey to pull it and no fruit and veg as yet. He guessed the animal would be stabled somewhere overnight and the merchandise either kept in that there dwelling or in a lock-up somewhere.

It was still early. Dawn had just broken and there was no sign of life from any of the dwellings as yet. He'd already worked out what he was going to say if asked. No one ought to recognise him in this neck of the woods anyway. Yes, that's what he'd tell them, he was looking for a man called John Griffin, an old relative of his, to tell him their cousin had passed away. Wouldn't sound too suspicious that.

He sat on a doorstep and watched the cellar entrance. At one point he almost dozed off and jerked to life when he heard voices. Pulling his flat cap a little over his face, he heard the following:

'Need to get to Covent Garden by seven this morning for the best prices. I was 'aving a word with a bloke there just yesterday, he had some great leafy cabbages and has promised me a good price. I'll drop them off at the stall later.'

The voice came from the shorter of three young men, all of whom looked very similar. Brothers, no doubt. All too old to be Tommy, who he'd been told was around twelve years of age.

'That's great, Billy!' Shouted one of them at the man who had spoken first.

The other two were pushing barrows across a cobbled area towards some sort of shed. He was right, it was some sort of lock-up. The one still stood by the cart clocked him for the first time and stared hard at him.

Bertie gulped but began walking towards him. 'Hello there. I'm wondering if you'd know a relative of mine from these parts called, John Griffin?'

The one who'd been called, Billy, shook his head. 'Sorry, can't say I have. How long ago was he living here?'

'Oh, about fifteen years ago. I haven't seen him in such a long time. You see, a relative of ours has passed away and I need to inform him of the funeral arrangements.'

Billy frowned. 'I can ask my Ma if you like? She knows everyone around here.'

Bertie was just about to decline the offer as he didn't want the woman brought into it as well, he might end up creating a right scene here if she then went and called on some neighbours, that was one way to be remembered. But before he had the chance to say "No, thank you", Billy had descended the cellar steps and was already summoning his mother.

It was only a couple of minutes until he was walking back up them with a middle-aged-looking woman in his wake. She looked a decent sort. Homely and kind. Stood behind her, was a young lad in a brown jacket and trousers and flat cap. Might that be Tommy? He looked the right sort of age.

'Hello, sir. I hear you're looking for a John Griffin who used to live in this area around fifteen years ago?'

Bertie nodded. 'Aye, that's right, ma'am.'

The woman rubbed her chin. 'Can't say I recognise the name and I've been living here nigh on twenty years. Are you sure you don't want Webber's Lane instead of Webber's Court?'

'Aye, that might be it. Maybe I've got the names mixed up.'

The young lad was now pulling on his mother's pinafore about to say something but his mother turned towards him and said, 'Go back inside, Tommy. I shan't be a tick.'

A result! So it was young Tommy after all. Now if he bided his time and waited until all three brothers were safely on their way to work, he could keep watch and tail young Tommy when he left his home.

***

Tailing the lad had been easier for Bertie at first. Initially, he'd stood on the corner out on the main thoroughfare and had appeared to be waiting for someone as he'd stood there hopping from foot to foot as though impatient. Strangely enough, it was where he, himself, had bumped into Angeline the other day. He cringed now when he thought how he'd treated his own daughter, shaking the living daylights out of her like that and all for a few measly pennies to spend at the pub. The poor girl had looked petrified right out of her wits. No wonder that family of his wanted no more to do with him.

The problem was when he was good he was very, very good and when he was bad he was horrid! He realised that too well. When the drink was in the wit was out. It was the alcohol that sent him spiralling into bad behaviour, just couldn't seem to help himself then.

As he stood in the doorway of the pub opposite keeping a watch on the boy, turning up the collar of his jacket and slipping down the peak of his flat cap so as not to be recognised by him, he wondered why he was doing this at all.

Then he reminded himself, he'd promised Eliza he'd help towards her wedding to George Whittle —the money would come in handy for that—after all, although he'd lost a lot in life, he still had his pride. As the father of the family, tradition warranted that the father of the bride paid out, but George, fair play to the young man, had said he was saving towards the day which would be a modest affair and towards enough rent money to put down for the next few months. A sensible young man was George.

Oh, now the lad was turning around and looking in every direction, checking out who was passing him. Disappointment was etched on his young face. Whoever he'd been waiting for he'd either missed or they were late or maybe didn't plan on showing at all.

A feeling of sympathy for the lad surged through his veins. He might have been his own son wedged in age between Sammy and Michael.

As he stood on the front step of the pub, the door opened as someone passed him to go inside. That familiar mingle of ale and tobacco came wafting towards him, tempting him to go in there. But no, he was on a mission and that was to follow young Tommy.

Drat! He stared across the road to where the lad had been stood earlier but he was no longer there. Surely he couldn't have got very far in a few seconds?

Ah, there he was ahead, just disappearing into the crowd. Dodging a couple of carts and a hansom cab, he crossed the busy thoroughfare and followed the lad. This time he wasn't going to take his eyes off Tommy Featherstone, not for a single second.

***

That was strange, young Tommy appeared to be heading towards the direction of Bow. What would he be going there for? Still, he carried on following him along the streets, ensuring he kept far back enough behind one or two folk so as not to get noticed by the lad. Then the game would be over.

Yes, he was definitely off to Bow as they passed familiar-looking streets. The old tannery, several pawn shops and pubs, until finally, the lad turned into a street of shops. This was Angeline's usual pitch to sell her matches near the Sampson's shop. And now the lad was headed towards that very same shop.

A coincidence? He thought not. No way would that boy walk all that distance from the Old Nichol to go in there on an errand for his ma or to purchase a packet of sweets. He narrowed his gaze. Of course! Angeline had been pitched in the Old Nichol that day where the lad had stood on the pavement earlier and now he had also turned up at her other pitch. Both he and Angeline now having

THE ANGEL OF CHRISTMAS ALLEY

a connection with this shop.

The Sampsons must have taken Arnold's nephew in there. Oh, this was going to be so easy, like taking sweets from a baby or should he say the Sampson's shop! Tommy had been gone for some time and when he peered inside the shop, Mr Sampson was busy serving a customer but there was no sign of Tommy Featherstone! He must have been taken into the living quarters by the shopkeeper's wife.

A slight pang of guilt prickled his conscience and told him to let sleeping dogs lie but then he thought of that gold sovereign Arnold Swindler had shown him with a promise of more to come if he got his nephew safely returned to him, no questions asked.

One thing that did concern him though was if the lad was still small enough to climb chimneys. He'd known of one lad who had become trapped and the chimney breast had to be knocked through to rescue him. Fortunately, the lad hadn't climbed too far and the sweep had managed to get him out unscathed, apart from ever after the lad having a bad attack of claustrophobia and he was never to climb another chimney after that.

It didn't sit right with him though about sending lads up chimneys these days not when there were special brushes that could be used. In any case, now it was against the law. But then again, if he asked no questions, it wasn't down to him what old Swindler did with his nephew after that. Maybe he was just concerned for the lad's welfare.

What puzzled him most though was how Angeline was caught up in this in the first place? What was her connection to Tommy? It mystified him, truth be told.

Bertie left the shop and waited in the shadows for the lad to emerge. He'd already been inside for around an hour or so. It was interesting to see who went in and out of the place. Young children after pokes of their favourite sweets, intense looking ladies with wicker baskets over their arms, no doubt after something for their husband's suppers, men coming out of there with pouches of tobacco to stuff their pipes with. All manner of life entered and emerged from there, particularly today. He hadn't realised it was such a busy shop. That Mr and Mrs Sampson must be rolling in it.

He yawned, this staking out business could get a bit boring at times as his eyelids fluttered shut from time to time with the monotony of it all.

Stay awake, Bertie, and you'll get your reward soon enough, it won't be in heaven though. But a few gold sovereigns for my time will do.

There was the sound of voices. A woman's and a lad's. It was her, the shopkeeper's wife. He narrowed his gaze to see Tommy beside her as though she were bidding him farewell. What was she saying to him? He strained to listen—all ears now.

'Now you go carefully, Tommy. You can call here

any time you like to see Bobby.' Then she handed him a paper poke of something he guessed were sweets. Not a bad outcome for the lad to get rewarded by the old biddy for visiting his friend. She was a kind-hearted sucker by the look of it. She stood on the doorstep to wave the lad off and then returned inside the shop as the overhead bell tinkled.

He'd wait a while until the lad reached the end of the street and then start to follow him again, reckoning that within around ten minutes or so he should be able to nab hold of him. He'd noticed a couple of discarded empty hessian sacks outside the Sampson shop where potatoes and carrots had been emptied inside a big wooden box for customers to choose for themselves. His idea was to capture the lad with a view to forcing him to lure Bobby out of the shop for him.

How careless of them not to take those sacks back inside the shop.

He crossed over the road and glancing right and left, picked one and walked off quickly with it. The lad was at the end of the road now, so he quickened his pace, his goal still in sight. He was walking at such a fast pace that Bertie was finding it difficult to keep up with him. Bertie's old arthritis was playing up something rotten of late, especially in this freezing cold weather.

'Blast it!' he cried out as he stumbled over an uneven section of the pavement. Pausing to draw a breath, he massaged his swollen knee. Luckily, he had managed to retain his balance there instead of hurtling through the air and landing flat on his face, that was the last thing he needed right now. The boy would be long gone at this rate if he wasn't careful, but then he noticed he'd paused outside that Goodman's pawn shop to gaze in the window. There'd been an eye-catching display in the window over the Christmas period which he guessed was still there. Two boxing monkeys worked by clockwork that made people laugh at their antics and at times, drew a small crowd of onlookers.

He was drawing near to the lad now. So close he could reach out and grab the collar of his jacket.

His quarry was in sight.

His arm reached out as he made to grasp him but his hand began to tremble as he did so. What was the matter with him? Was he losing his nerve or was it because he'd weaned himself off the bottle this past few days and he was having a bad attack of *delirium tremens* otherwise known as the DTs or shakes?

Whatever it was, it felt as though his hand no longer belonged to him.

He drew in a deep composed breath and tried to reach out again with the same effect.

Then the lad turned and catching sight of him, smiled up at him.

'Great, ain't they, mister?' He chuckled at the monkeys' antics as they took punches at one another, somersaulted and ended up lying on the floor only to spring into action and do the same thing all over again. That was good, the brief glance the lad had of him early that morning when he'd spoken to his family, hadn't registered with him.

'Er yes, lad. They are very comical!'

He noticed Tommy had the cutest smile and for a moment his heart went out to him. Why? Because he might be one of his own sons standing there enjoying that scene—Sammy or Michael. It wasn't the lad's fault any of this, he'd just got caught up in it all. In any case, his real quarry was hidden well away from the world in the Sampson's living quarters. What could this little rascal do for him? If he kidnapped him to lure that Bobby one out of the shop it might not work as the lad no doubt had his loyalties towards him. No, he was going to just have to play the long game and kidnap Bobby himself. Quite how he was going to do that, he just didn't know.

***

When Michael returned home from work that evening, Angeline had a pot of corned beef stew bubbling away on the stove. She'd made it go a little further by making some suet dumplings to go along with it. Working it out, she'd made seven dumplings, so they could have one each, with an extra for Michael as he did such physical, demanding work. He smiled broadly as he entered the house.

'Something smells good!' he enthused. Then

noticing the look on Angeline's face he asked, 'What's wrong?'

'It's Ma. Eliza had to leave here for a while this morning while I was out and Ma left the house.'

Michael shook his head. 'I didn't think Ma would be capable in her condition. Where is she now?'

'She's been in bed since the middle of the day, sleeping it all off.'

Michael's forehead creased into a furrowed frown. 'Sleeping what off?'

'She got as far as the Kings Arms and went in and bought a bottle of gin.'

Michael's eyes widened. 'Oh no. Not again.'

'Thankfully, she hadn't finished the bottle when I found her out in the yard as if she'd just come from the privy.'

'You think she would have drunk it all otherwise if you'd not found her?'

'Yes, I do. She's so upset about this pregnancy. I think she thought drinking a full bottle of gin and taking a hot bath, would get rid of the baby for good.'

'I can't believe Ma would do such a thing,' Michael said shaking his head in disbelief, 'she's always been such a loving mother to us all.'

'She's not the same though, Michael. Not since working at that match factory. It all began back then when she got taken sick. Her body is too weak to carry a baby. She might lose it in any case.' He nodded with understanding. 'Anyhow, I'm getting the doctor out first thing in the morning just to check her over.'

'That sounds a good idea. I'm sorry I'm not here more often to keep an eye on her.'

'Please,' she laid a reassuring hand on his arm, 'don't blame yourself. You need that job. We all rely on you as you're the main breadwinner these days, not that no mark of a father of ours. Do you know Eliza and George have actually been to see him to ask for permission to marry?'

Michael stroked his stubbled chin. He tended to sprout a five o'clock shadow by the time he returned home in the evenings. 'No. I didn't know that. Look on the bright side though, Eliza is a bone idle madam, there'll be one less mouth to feed when she's left here.'

She supposed her brother made a good point. 'At least she is trying though.'

'Yes, very trying!' chuckled Michael as he wrapped his arm around his sister. 'I don't know what we'd all do without you, Angeline, our angel of the home.'

Angeline's lips curved into a nervous smile. Sometimes she wished life could be more carefree for her, instead of having the weight of the family's affairs on her young shoulders.

Chapter Thirteen

When Doctor Montague arrived at Angeline's home the following day, she thought he looked ever so tired going by the dark circles beneath his eyes. He apologised as soon as he entered the house, removing his hat, scarf and coat and handing them to her. She hung his coat and scarf behind the door and placed his hat on the table.

The doctor shook his head. 'I am so sorry about yesterday, I was up to my neck in it as the other doctor I work with was away. He's returned now so my workload shouldn't be so great today.'

'That's all right, Doctor,' she smiled. 'I'm just glad you've arrived. What would your fee for a call out be?'

'Let me be the judge of that and what's necessary for your mother,' he replied curtly, causing her to gulp with fear in case she didn't have enough money. She had the sixpenny piece from yesterday and Michael had handed her a shilling, but she also had a few pennies from yesterday's work. She hadn't been able to go to her usual pitch as yet today as she thought it more important for Ma to be attended to. Eliza had gone to queue up at the factory for more materials necessary for matchmaking this time without complaint.

'Upstairs, is she?' The doctor asked, glancing at the ceiling.

'Yes, Doctor.' Angeline began to ascend the narrow, curved stone stairs with the doctor in tow. He was quite a tall chap so she realised it must be hard for him having to stoop a little, but he said nothing.

When she reached the landing she tapped softly on Ma's bedroom door. 'Ma, I've got Doctor Montague with me.'

Ma answered with a weak, thin voice. 'Do come in.'

The room was dark when they entered and immediately, Angeline rushed over to the window to pull open the drapes. Why hadn't she thought of doing this earlier when she'd given her mother a good wash all down and dressed her in a clean nightdress? But it was still pitch black outside then and she just hadn't thought about it as her mother had drifted off back to sleep.

'Now then,' said Doctor Montague, as he placed his bag on a chair near the bed and rolled up his shirt sleeves to the elbow, 'I understand you're pregnant and you've still got that harsh cough, have you?'

'Yes, Doctor,' said Ma, who had seemed to come to life now as she sat herself up in the bed.

The doctor turned away to search his leather bag for his stethoscope and then faced them to ask Angeline to lift Ma's nightdress while he listened to her breathing and palpated her abdomen. But what he said next, floored the pair of them.

'This sickness you've been getting, Mrs Barker, comes and goes does it?'

'Yes,' Ma nodded. 'It's been happening for months, Doctor. But has got particularly bad lately.'

He lifted his eyebrows. 'And your cough? Has that improved at all?'

'No.' She shook her head. 'Is there a tonic you can give me, Doctor? To help with the sickness, like? And maybe a cough medicine that might work better than the other I've been taking?'

The doctor looked at Ma with a great deal of sympathy in his eyes. 'I've seen these symptoms before, especially with women and girls who live in this area. You worked at the Bryant and May match factory for a spell, didn't you, Mrs Barker?'

Ma nodded. 'Yes, I did. I was there for a year or so until ill health caused me to quit.'

'That ill health you speak of was probably caused by the phosphorus in the match-making process. Did you handle the stuff very much?'

'Yes, I had to I worked on the dipping machine and there was a lot of the white powder around the place too on workstations and such. Often we were made to eat our sandwiches at our stations, which hadn't been cleaned up.'

'That explains things then,' nodded the doctor. 'You have phosphorus poisoning, Mrs Barker.'

'But I thought I was one of the lucky ones as

I didn't have that phossy jaw condition like many get.'

'Lucky in that respect maybe, but unlucky in another. It's gone to your lungs and I fear to your liver too.'

'But the baby! What about the baby!' cried Ma now becoming animated with anxiety.

'I'd wager there is no baby, Mrs Barker. I think the nausea and vomiting is because your liver is breaking down and it's caused your stomach to swell slightly.'

'But is there anything that can be done for Ma's condition, Doctor?' asked Angeline, desperate now to find some sort of help for her mother.

'Nothing that can make her better as such, but I can prescribe laudanum for her which will alleviate her pain and I can give her some medicine that will help with the sickness though not prevent it entirely.'

Angeline felt the bedroom spin, this couldn't be happening, not to her lovely mother. The woman who had fought all these years until now to keep her family together. The woman who had put up with Pa's behaviour all this time and given up her music hall career at his request.

The doctor indicated with his eyes by glancing at the door, that he needed to speak to Angeline outside.

'We won't be long, Ma,' Angeline said to her mother, gently patting her hand. Ma nodded but now appeared to have a catatonic stare as she attempted to process all the doctor had told her.

Once outside the room, Angeline closed the door behind them as the doctor whispered.

'She has a few months at most. Just keep her comfortable and give her the laudanum whenever she needs it. Though it's quite addictive, so space out doses and if I were you, keep it where she can't get at it herself nor the children, as in the wrong hands, an overdose could prove lethal.'

Angeline nodded. It was all starting to sound so serious but after what the doctor had said, it was all beginning to make sense. Ma had been fit as a flea before working at that match factory. Her cough had developed about six months after beginning work there. No wonder she hadn't wanted either of her daughters to work there, even though they'd asked.

Doctor Montague handed her a note to take to the chemist for both medicines. 'Thank you, Doctor. How much do I owe you?'

He waved a hand in her direction. 'Nothing on this occasion. Save your money for the medicine,' he said, as he placed a hand on her shoulder.

Angeline couldn't believe the kindness of the man, her bottom lip trembled as she began to weep. He'd realised the family were in financial trouble and didn't want to make things worse for them all by charging a fee for visiting Ma.

'Ssh, there now. Don't let your mother know how upset you are, you need to be strong for her, Angeline.'

She gazed at the doctor through blurred eyes and forced a smile as she nodded.

The next few months were going to be the hardest months she had ever known in her young life.

***

When the doctor had departed, Angeline sat on the bed and held her mother's hand until she drifted off to sleep, all the while mulling over the situation. She finally decided to tell Eliza and Michael first and Sammy and Joanna later. She was going to have to put it to the little ones in the best way she knew how and say Ma was going to join the angels in heaven soon, but that one day they'd see her again. Tears pricked the back of her eyes at the thought of it. She just couldn't bear the idea of life without her mother.

Before the doctor departed, she'd told him about Ma's alcohol dependency and he said that sadly, that too, would have an effect on her liver and maybe would have shortened her life even further.

By the time, Eliza returned home, Angeline was all cried out, feeling that she could hardly think any more, her mind numb from taking everything in, after all, what she'd been expecting was for the doctor to confirm her mother was having a baby and maybe to give her some new medicine for that cough of hers—not to explain that shortly she was to meet her maker.

Life could be so cruel. Although Ma looked old and worn out these days, in reality, she might have had a lot of life to live and a lot of love to give. Now all her hopes and dreams for all her tomorrows would be crushed. There were few tomorrows left.

As soon as Eliza caught sight of her sister's face, she realised something was wrong. 'Your eyes are so puffy, Angeline. You've been crying. What's wrong? Is it the rent man hounding us again?'

Angeline shook her head. She had hoped to tell her older brother and sister the news at the same time but she couldn't hold back. 'Sit down, I have something to tell you,' she said in a trembling voice.

Eliza, without even removing her shawl, placed down her matchmaking cardboard box containing the glue and twine in the middle of the table and took a seat as Angeline sat opposite. She stretched across the table to take her sister's hand, almost instinctively.

'W...what's going on?' Eliza sounded fearful now.

Angeline swallowed hard. 'The doctor called here earlier and Ma's not pregnant as she thought she was.'

'Well, that's good, ain't it?' Eliza's voice was artificially high.

'Yes, in one respect but not in another.'

Eliza shook her head. 'I don't understand?'

'Ma may not be pregnant but she has got something wrong with her lungs and liver. She's been poisoned by the phosphorus from the match factory.'

Hearing that, Eliza glared at the box in front of her. 'B...but she'll be all right, won't she? There's some medicine she can take for it?'

Angeline shook her head. 'The swelling on Ma's stomach and the nausea and vomiting are from her illness not from having a baby. Doctor Montague thinks she's only got months left to live and all we can do is to keep her as comfortable as possible. I have to nip across to the pharmacy to fetch her some laudanum and medicine to help with the sickness. I didn't want to leave her unattended after what happened yesterday.'

Eliza's eyes were glistening with tears now and one large one fell on the cardboard box on the table. She sniffed loudly. 'But it can't be true. I don't want it to be.' She began to get hysterical as she raised her voice and started to scream.

Angeline stood and going across to her sister slapped her cheek causing her head to whip back but it shocked her and brought her back to reality as she rubbed her reddened cheek.

'I'm sorry I had to do that, Eliza. I was shocked as you are, and still am. But I can't have you screaming hysterically like a raving banshee and waking up Ma. She needs to rest, now more than ever. If she wakes now she might be in some discomfort and I've not got the laudanum as yet. Now I'm trusting you to listen out for her when I'm gone. Whatever you do, *do not* leave her alone. If she goes out drinking again, it might be the end of her.'

Eliza nodded vacantly, dabbing at her runny nose with a handkerchief. 'I'll be all right,' she said, her voice thick now. Angeline's heart went out to the girl and she hugged her warmly towards her, then reseated herself.

'Does Michael know yet?' Eliza blinked back her tears.

'No, he doesn't. We shall tell him together this evening. Then afterwards I'll explain in simple terms to Sammy and Joanna.'

'That's the best idea as they're too young to understand very much.'

Angeline, though, knew the pair realised *something* was wrong of late with Ma being confined to her bed most of the time. The last time they'd seen her go outdoors was that Christmas Eve Pa had dragged them all out Carol singing.

Eliza sniffed loudly, causing her sister to jolt out of her reverie. 'I've just thought of something...'

'Oh?' Angeline's brow lifted.

'I can't possibly get married now, the wedding will have to be postponed with Ma so sick.'

'I think the opposite. You should marry before...'

Angeline didn't even need to say the words they both realised she meant before Ma died.

And in that moment, tears streamed down their cheeks.

'Can you bring the wedding forward even?' Angeline said finally.

'I'll have a word with George and see what we

can do.'

Angeline reached out and touched her sister's hand in a mark of sympathy. In that moment, they became as close as a pair of sisters could ever be.

Chapter Fourteen

The following day, Eliza made her way to find her father who had now taken a room at the Kings Arms. She wondered if he was holed up with the floozie who had helped to break up their family? Was she living on the premises?

As she entered the pub's barroom, she almost gagged from the smell of strong pipe tobacco from a couple of old men who were playing cards in the corner, shrouded by the wispy grey smoke. She blew out a hard breath when to her relief, she realised the barmaid in question wasn't there. Instead, behind the bar was a man with a bald head and thick bushy sideburns. The landlord, she expected. Maybe only one person was needed at this early hour of the day. The man was drying a tankard with a cloth as she approached and looking up, he smiled and said, 'What can I do for you, young miss?'

Eliza smiled and cleared her throat before speaking. 'I've come to see my father, Bertie Barker. Is he here?'

'Aye,' the man, who seemed to have some sort of northern accent to her ears, nodded. 'He's up yon stairs. Maybe I can bring him down to you?'

'I have something to say to him of a private nature and I ain't too sure we might not be overheard downstairs,' she said, glancing around nervously as a couple of more men drifted into the pub.

'I quite understand thee,' he said, tapping the side of his nose with his index finger. Then he opened a hatch door on the side of the wooden bar to allow her access. 'Follow me, miss.'

He led her to a small corridor behind the bar area then he pointed to a flight of stairs. 'His room is up there, second on the right.'

She thanked him and gingerly, lifting her skirts made her way upstairs. The landing was low-ceilinged and dark with a faint hint of a damp smell. She found the correct door and lifting her fist, knocked on it.

'Whatcha want?' bellowed out a voice.

She guessed maybe he was worried in case some creditor or another was after him for money, so had to take care answering. 'It's me, Pa. Eliza,' she said softly.

Immediately, the door swung open and her father's face split into a wide grin.

'Well, if it ain't my favourite girl!' He said as he embraced her warmly. She knew she was the only child of his who wanted to see him right now and although he'd hurt her too by going off with that floozie barmaid, he was still her Pa. Nothing would ever change that.

Before closing the door, he glanced up and down

the corridor and when satisfied, shut it behind them. 'Now then, what brings you to see me, darlin'?'

She glanced around the shabby little room, which to her seemed worse than her own home. It was just one room with a small table with some unwashed crockery still upon it, a rickety-looking chair by the side of that, a pallet bed laid unmade in the corner and the fire in the hearth was unlit. Even the wallpaper in the room seemed to have given up the ghost as it had peeled off part of the walls. So cold looking. Stark.

Drawing in a breath and letting it out again, she said, 'It's me wedding, Pa. It's got to be brought forward.'

He narrowed his gaze as he stared at her and she just knew what he was thinking.

'Oh no, nothing like that,' she reassured, shaking her head. 'I ain't pregnant or anything. It's Ma.'

'Your mother? What's up? Take a seat.' He gestured towards the table with his hand.

Gingerly, she drew out the chair from the table hoping it wouldn't collapse beneath her, but as she sat it seemed stable enough, her father remained standing.

She raised her chin and looked up at him. 'Angeline got the doctor out yesterday. Ma thought she was having a baby...'

Her father gulped as his face reddened. 'A baby?'

'She's not. I wish that's all it was. She's been

THE ANGEL OF CHRISTMAS ALLEY

getting sick lately.'

'The coughing? Aye, I know all about that, she was coughing her guts up before I left.'

'It's not just the coughing, her stomach got bigger and she was vomiting too, that's why she thought she was having a baby.'

He was looking concerned now. 'So, if she's not pregnant and you say she's sick, then what is it, Eliza?'

Eliza shook her head as her eyes filled up with tears. 'She's dying, Pa. She's not got much time left to live.'

He shot her a curious smile and then huffed out a chuckle. 'No, you're pulling me leg, gal. You always were a bit of a prankster.'

'No, Pa,' she sniffed. 'Would I be crying like this if it were all some joke?'

'B…but tell me what the doctor said?'

'She's been poisoned from that match factory. The phosphorus powder has got to her lungs and her liver.'

'That damn factory!' he yelled, his eyes widening now, the whites on show.

Eliza gasped when he thumped his fist down on the table, causing a teacup to rattle in its saucer as she flinched.

Composing herself after her father's outburst, she said, 'So, that's the reason George and I need to get wed, for Ma's sake, before she passes over as I realise how happy it would make her to see me settled down. I have to go to see him after calling here, but I thought you should know.' She stood and touched her father's shoulder, leaning in to kiss him softly on the cheek, his eyes now brimming with tears too.

Then she turned her back and walked silently from the room. What more could she say? There was no magic pill Ma could take to make her all better again and she realised her father now had his conscience to contend with.

Chapter Fifteen

Eliza and George called to see the vicar of the local church and explained the circumstances to him. The Reverend John Bartholomew Aylward was more than happy to comply with the couple's request for an early wedding, and he scheduled the ceremony to take place in three weeks' time. He explained the reason for this was that the banns, which were a legal requirement, needed to be read out in church for three consecutive weeks. Eliza had no idea what on earth "the banns" meant before the Reverend's explanation.

The vicar was a jolly person who well understood the solemnity of it all and he offered to visit Ma at home. He suggested as she was so sick that the wedding ceremony take place initially in the privacy of the home, followed by a later blessing at the church itself. This seemed to make everyone concerned happy, all except Pa that was.

Since hearing the news about his wife's health and soon-to-be demise, he seemed to shut down and took to the ale again.

'It's all my damn fault!' he was heard to say to fellow drinkers at the Kings Arms. He'd cut off all contact with the barmaid in question, much to her dismay and now he wandered around the streets like a helpless vagrant, unkempt and uncared for.

But one day after a chat in a pub with a fellow he knew, the man put the idea into his mind that maybe if he got together enough money then he could take his wife to Harley Street in London to seek a cure for her sickness. To do that, he badly needed that bag of gold sovereigns from Mr Swindler. Somehow he was going to have to get his mitts on Bobby Swindler and return him to his uncle.

***

Angeline wiped her mother's fevered brow with a wet flannel. 'Sssh, Ma. Try to get some sleep,' she reassured.

Ma muttered something that sounded muffled to her ears. Something like, 'Tell them, I'm on my way...' but she couldn't be sure that's what she'd said at all. Wringing out the flannel into the metal bowl, she placed it on her mother's forehead. She needed to sleep if she was to be ready for this wedding tomorrow. That's if she could manage to stay conscious.

Quietly, Angeline closed the bedroom door, turning the knob until the door clicked, to be met with Eliza standing behind her.

'How's Ma in there?'

Angeline shook her head and then bit her lower lip. 'She's not too good. To be honest with you I don't know how she'll stay awake for the ceremony tomorrow. It's all the laudanum I suppose. Doctor

Montague increased the dose yesterday to help her cope with the pain.'

Angeline could sense her sister was now near to tears to hear this news. 'Oh,' she said, pressing the back of her hand to her forehead. 'I should never have insisted we rush the wedding. I just thought...'

'I know what you thought,' said Angeline kindly, 'that Ma would get some happiness to see you were happy and settled before she passes over to the other side.'

Eliza nodded. 'Now though, I feel it ain't worth all the trouble as I'm making things worse.' She turned towards her sister and Angeline hugged her. It was becoming difficult trying to support everyone. Not only did she bear the main brunt of supporting her mother but there were the little ones and Michael too. Everyone seemed to view her as the little mother of the house now when at her age she ought to be without a care in the world.

'Did you get to speak to Pa?' Angeline asked, now drawing away from the embrace.

'Yes, he said he'll come to the wedding but when I called around again yesterday, there was a strong smell of alcohol on his breath. I think he's taken it hard about Ma. He asked can he see her after the wedding on his own. But I don't know if that's such a good idea, do you?'

'I don't know either.' Angeline's forehead puckered into a frown, then the creases smoothed out as she added, 'perhaps leave that decision up to

Ma?'

'You're right. It's Ma's choice whether she wants to see him or not and whether she's forgiven him. He's given up that floozie one an' all.'

Angeline's eyebrows shot up in surprise. That, she did not know. 'He's hurt us all for sure, particularly Ma. And I don't think Michael will forgive him in a hurry. I'm a bit concerned he'll go for him at the wedding.'

Eliza huffed out a breath. 'No, he won't do that. I've had a word with him and he says out of respect for Ma and the little ones, he'll stay well clear.'

'That's good then.'

Eliza placed her hand on Angeline's shoulder. 'Will you help put rags in me hair tonight? I want it to look lovely for tomorrow.'

'Of course I will and I'll help you wash it as well.'

That night, Angeline helped Eliza prepare for the following day, winding her sister's hair up securely and tying it with pieces of old material that had been cut up into strips and now referred to as "rags".

Eliza seemed tentative and Angeline wondered if it was because she was now leaving the family home as well as getting wed. George had arranged with his parents that they would move in with them. It would be a squash for the family as he still had two younger brothers at home but at least the rooms were bigger than at the Barker's household. There was a parlour room that was kept for best as Mrs Whittle was quite houseproud;

it was the room most people kept pristine for special occasions like Christmas and would even be used for funerals for some families where the loved ones coffin would be on display before laying them to rest. But in this case, it was to be turned into a bedroom and living room for the newlyweds. There wouldn't be a honeymoon as such as they were saving their pennies but George had promised a day trip somewhere, maybe into the city when the weather improved. Eliza had spoken of them going to one of those fancy tea rooms and maybe taking a stroll around Hyde Park. Even seeing Buckingham Palace! And when she'd spoken of these things, her eyes had glittered with the excitement of it all. Yet, Angeline realised behind it was an immeasurable sadness.

When everyone was in bed that night, Ma's best dress having been laid out for the following day with plans to help her downstairs for the ceremony, Angeline held her sister's hand in bed. It would be the last time she'd get to do this. Tomorrow that spot would be taken by Joanna who would be sleeping there instead. The girl was growing up fast and it had been decided that she should no longer share with her younger brother as she was developing into a young lady, especially after Ma's suggestion at Christmas that all the boys share a room and the girls another. Of course, as Ma was so sick, she needed her privacy and a room of her own.

It would be a long time before either sister got

to sleep that night but eventually, they drifted off realising that many changes were about to take place.

Chapter Sixteen

The first thing Angeline heard when she woke up was her father's voice down below. What on earth was he doing here already? Had she overslept? She glanced to look across at her sister, but her side of the bed was empty. Then she realised it was Eliza their father was speaking to in the living room.

Hastily, she dressed and walked downstairs to hear Pa's voice getting increasingly louder as Eliza stood in his path, blocking him from getting to the stairway. Angeline managed to slip past and stood beside her sister.

'What's going on?' She demanded as she folded her arms.

'Yer'll let me past, won't you, darlin'?' he said with a sly grin on his face.

But all Angeline could think about was that time he'd shaken her like an apple tree out on the street, causing her to stumble backwards. The fear she'd felt at the time. Now though, she no longer feared her father, seeing him as a flawed individual who'd lost those who ought to have been held dear to him.

'What is it you want?' With arms folded, she tapped her foot and gritted her teeth.

'Just want you girls to lemme pass to go upstairs to see your mother, 'tis all.'

'Oh no, you're flamin' not!' yelled Eliza her eyes flashing in anger. 'And after the show this morning, you're not coming to this wedding either. You've been drinking again.'

One look at their father's flushed face and bloodshot eyes could tell anyone that. His clothing appeared dishevelled as if he was wearing what he'd slept in last night, and he stank to high heaven of alcohol.

Angeline was about to say something when the front door was thrust open, both girls turned their heads to see Michael standing there with a pile of small logs in his arms, ready to light the fire.

'What's *he* doing here?' he said angrily.

'N...now, now,' said their father, holding up the palms of his hands as though in surrender. 'I come to make peace not war. I just want to speak to your mother, that's all. Tell her how sorry I am and to check how she's doing.' His bottom lip was quivering now.

Angeline couldn't tell if that was from fear of Michael's reaction or upset about Ma's terminal illness.

There was an impasse as Michael stooped to stack the logs beside the hearth, then he stood and walked towards their father and taking the man by the collar of his jacket in both his hands, he shook him roughly. For the first time, Angeline noticed that Michael was now taller than Pa and Pa had noticed it too as his eyes enlarged and his mouth fell open at the shock of it all.

There was some satisfaction now that her brother was doing the same to Pa that Pa had done to her on that street corner. It was like a taste of his own medicine.

'Now, get out of here!' Michael yelled as he pressed his face towards his father's. Then he pushed him away.

'B...but who will give Eliza away if I leave?'

'I will,' said Michael, gazing at his sister with pride. 'I will and shall be proud to do so. We don't want you spoiling her day or upsetting Ma today of all days.'

Bertie Barker knew when he was defeated. Nodding slowly, head down, he made for the front door, then paused to turn and focus his gaze on all three of them. 'I do regret my selfish behaviour, you know. I am going to change. I've let you all down, I know I have.'

For a moment, it appeared as though Eliza was about to say something maybe to stop him from leaving but Michael shook his head at her as if to say, 'No, don't!'

Turning for a final time, Pa walked through the front door.

Angeline puffed out a breath of relief while Eliza broke down in tears as the door clicked shut. Pa had done it again—upset them all on another special occasion. Thank goodness Ma and the two younger ones were still in bed.

***

It was some time until Eliza composed herself from the upset of it all. Trembling, and with tears in her eyes, she looked at her brother. 'I don't know if this ought to go ahead, perhaps I should call it all off...'

'Don't be foolish, Eliza,' he said, placing the palms of his hands on her shoulders and gazing into her eyes. 'If you do that, Pa will have won. It's as though he loves to ruin things for his family.'

'Michael's right,' added Angeline. 'Go ahead and marry George today. We'll have some breakfast and then I'll help you to get ready for your big day.'

Eliza nodded with tears in her eyes as Michael took a step back.

'And I'll be a very proud brother giving you away today,' he enthused.

Following a light breakfast, Eliza was more herself again, even if she was all cried out and Angeline could have flamin' thumped her father for upsetting her sister. Even though it was evident she was his favourite, he was so selfish that he wouldn't think twice about putting himself first, even before her. His idea had been to see Ma and get close to her again, there was no doubt about that just to ease his conscience.

Angeline helped her sister by removing the tightly wound rags from her hair and brushing it until it shone. Then she pinned it up in a pretty fashion so that soft tendrils framed her sister's elfin face. And with her Sunday best floral dress on, the one with the lace collar, she thought she'd never seen Eliza look more beautiful than she did right now.

**

Reverend Aylward arrived in plenty of time to speak with Eliza before the ceremony, whilst Angeline washed and dressed Ma.

'I think I'll wear the frock I wore for me own wedding day,' said Ma in a weak tone of voice.

Angeline blinked. 'Are you sure, Ma? You told me that one no longer fits you.' The truth was, she didn't want to be reminded that her mother had once married her father, not today at any rate. That their lovely mother had once had hopes and dreams for the future, just like Eliza did today. But all Ma's hopes and dreams had been dashed by marrying Albert Barker who had convinced her to stop singing on stage and instead, to give her time to a houseful of children. The biggest child of all though was Pa himself. He'd given their mother more grief than any of her children ever had.

'Yes, I'm sure. I've lost so much weight it should fit me now.'

And Ma was right, even though her belly was swollen from her liver complaint, Angeline was able to ease the light blue cotton dress with its frilled bodice easily over her head. It looked a little young now for a woman of her age, but she wasn't going to tell her mother that. It was pretty and probably the nicest dress Ma had ever owned.

And if it brought her pleasure, who was she to complain?

'There's something else...' said Ma.

Angeline raised an eyebrow. 'What is it?'

When you're laying out the wedding breakfast here later, use my special tablecloth, the one I told you to use at Christmas and the best china cups as well.'

She nodded at her mother. It was almost as if Ma was recreating her own wedding day to Pa.

This would probably be the last celebratory occasion Ma would ever attend and Angeline intended to make it special both for her and Eliza. Mrs Featherstone had baked one of her special cakes for it. The wedding cakes at the bakery would have been a bit too expensive for them to afford.

So, they were all set for Eliza's wedding. All they needed now was the groom.

***

The ticking of the mantel clock seemed to get louder with each tick as Eliza, Michael, Angeline, Ma, the vicar and both younger children sat and waited. The service was supposed to take place at ten o'clock at the house and the blessing afterwards at the church an hour later. Only Eliza, George, and Reverend Aylward would be going there, Michael would be off to work, the children going to school, late with special permission and Angeline was taking the day off from selling her matches to care for Ma.

It had been decided that while Ma was sick, Eliza would still assemble her matchboxes at the house while keeping an eye on Ma when Angeline was at her pitch. Then in the afternoon, she'd return to the Whittle's house to tend to her husband.

Today, George had to work for a few hours before being allowed special leave. Angeline glanced at Eliza who was fidgeting with her handkerchief in her hand.

'I expect he's late as it's hard for him to get away on time,' Angeline reassured, so as not to unduly worry her sister.

'These things happen,' said the reverend stoically. 'Look, it doesn't matter if George is delayed today as I've not got any services after the church blessing until six o'clock tonight.'

Eliza nodded gratefully, but Angeline could tell by the way her sister was now tugging on her handkerchief, how concerned she was.

Was she thinking he wouldn't show up at all? He'd never let her down before. But then again, there was always a first time. And last.

'He'll be here,' said Michael. 'And if he doesn't arrive in the next ten minutes or so then I shall go and look for him.' He placed a comforting hand on Eliza's shoulder.

Then to break the tense moment, Angeline said, 'Let's all have a cup of tea while we wait, shall we?'

'That's a good idea,' said Ma, who looked concerned herself now. 'A very good idea indeed.'

After they'd finished their cups of tea, Michael

donned his cap and jacket and made his way to the door, turning, he looked at Eliza and said, 'I'm going to see if I can find him for you.'

Eliza nodded as she tried to stem the tears as Angeline held her hand.

What if Michael couldn't find him? What then? Would they have to send the vicar away?

Less than fifteen minutes had passed before the door swung open and with a big grin on his face, Michael declared, 'The groom's here!'

And behind him, limped George looking quite abashed. 'I'm so sorry everyone, especially to you, Eliza.'

'It doesn't matter, all that matters is that you're here now. But do you still want to marry me?' she blinked.

Cradling her face in his hands, he paused to gaze into her eyes. 'Of course I do. Let's get wed and I can explain later.'

***

'*I George Henry Whittle, take thee, Elizabeth Mary Barker, to be my wedded wife, to have and to hold from this day forward, for better, for worse, for richer, for poorer, in sickness and in health…*'

Angeline watched her sister marry George through glassy eyes. The service was beautiful, simply beautiful. Although she'd chastised Eliza more often than not for going off to meet George when there was work to be done, she realised he'd take very good care of her sister. And standing here right now, she knew how much they loved one another and how happy they were together.

Ma watched from the armchair, well-cushioned with pillows from her bed and a thick blanket over her legs. She had a big smile on her face. It was the most animated Angeline had seen her mother in ever such a long time.

It transpired that George had injured his foot unloading a small packing crate at the docks. Fortunately, after being seen by the company's doctor, it was deemed not to be too serious. It had been cleaned and dressed and now just a little rest for a couple of days was all that was required. It made Eliza realise though how dangerous her new husband's occupation might be.

Before the couple left to go to the church for a blessing where George's family would be waiting in attendance, Michael raised a glass of sherry as a toast, a bottle they'd been gifted from his employer.

'Here's to Mr and Mrs Whittle. God bless them both!"

They all cheered as Angeline thought: *God bless us all!*

Chapter Seventeen

It was that very same day of the wedding when Bertie had been told to leave the family home that something strange happened to him. He'd been walking along Christmas Alley, blethering to himself how unfair it was to be shown the door by Michael and how he'd been prevented from seeing his wife by his very own offspring when although there was no one else around, he had the sensation of being followed by someone. But every time he turned around, there was no one there.

Initially, he'd thought that maybe it was Michael come after him to warn him off, but no, he'd turn and all he'd see behind him was the cobbled path and in the distance, the arch that led on to Victoria Street. Feeling the drink had addled his senses, he shook his head. The best thing now was to get back to his digs and drink a couple of pints of water and not ale, and sleep it all off.

Then he felt it, a strange sensation as though someone had walked over his grave as the hairs on the back of his neck prickled.

'Who is it?' he yelled, frightened now, spinning around in a circular motion to ensure he didn't miss some threat towards his safety. 'Who's there?

I ain't got no money...'

It was almost a whisper of a voice. 'Albert! Albert!'

The voice sounded like his own dear mother's but she had passed on many a year since he was a young lad.

Then he saw it when he turned, a ball of light, so bright it might have been the sun for it dazzled him and he fell to his knees, shielding his eyes with the back of his arm from its powerful rays.

'What is it you want from me?' he demanded.

'It's not what *I* want from you,' the voice whispered softly, 'it's what your family needs from *you*.'

'They don't want me,' he was weeping now.

'You're wrong, Albert. They need you now.'

'They won't forgive me after all I've done...' he was weeping openly now.

'In whom we have redemption through his blood, the forgiveness of sins, according to the riches of his grace...'

Bertie moved his arm away from his eyes and was now to his surprise, able to withstand the light. Now it seemed comforting. 'I'm not past forgiveness, then?'

'No, you are not. There's still time to make amends if you truly want to.'

Shaking his head in perplexity, he fought to think what he ought to do and turned away for a moment. He loved his family and hadn't intended to put them through all of this. Yes, that's what he'd do for the first step. Eliza and George were due to have a blessing later at that church. He'd go home now and get tidied up and sober up. Then he'd return and ask them if they minded him being there. He'd make a start, they could only say no.

He turned back towards the light to answer, but it was no longer there. Rubbing his eyes, he wondered if he'd imagined the whole thing? If anyone were to see him on his knees in the alleyway they'd wonder what on earth was going on.

Puffing, he hauled himself up onto his feet and made his way from the alley. He was going to keep his promise. But to whom? That ball of light, who was it? An angel? The good Lord himself? An apparition? Whom or whatever, it wasn't too late to make good.

He ran towards his digs with extreme purpose now, intending to have a good wash and something to eat and drink. Hopefully, he'd make it to the church on time, clean, presentable and sober.

***

Being stood in the graveyard was sobering enough though, Bertie thought as he glanced at the various headstones around him, some tilted at varying angles and others covered in strands of ivy, coated with a covering of frost. Several of the occupants he noticed, had died far too young.

The end of us all.

Now he had a chance to make amends, living

out the rest of his life doing good instead of bad. Whatever that had been that happened to him in the alleyway, whether real or imagined was an epiphany of sorts for him. He'd finally been brought to his senses and seen the error of his ways.

'Pa?'

Eliza's voice shook him out of his reverie as she blinked several times at the disbelief of seeing her father now standing in front of her outside the church, all spruced up sober.

'Yes, it's really me,' he smiled. 'Sorry for letting you down earlier but I'm here now if you'll allow me to attend?'

Eliza exchanged uncertain glances with George, who finally nodded his approval. After all, he hadn't bore witness to the earlier fracas at the house and Eliza did appear to want to think the best of him. Maybe he didn't deserve a second chance from any of them but the one most likely to give it was his dear Eliza. Maybe if he conducted himself well here, it would be a start. A new beginning for them all.

He assumed that was Mr and Mrs Whittle stood at the church entrance, he hadn't met them as yet, but surely they would already have formed a bad opinion of him if his daughter had told them how he'd abandoned his family over Christmas and what the circumstances might be?

But that wasn't the case as the pair greeted him warmly. Jemima Whittle being short and widegirthed compared to his wife, Mavis, who was tall and spindly. Henry Whittle was a portly sort of chap with red, flushed cheeks. Bertie immediately took to the pair, which was unusual for him as he was usually so suspicious of strangers.

The best part for Bertie was escorting Eliza, and although she'd already legally wed George back at the house, he still asked the vicar if he might walk her down the aisle and much to his pleasure, he was allowed that privilege.

Afterwards, stood outside the church, Eliza leaned into her father and pecking a kiss on his cheek, said, 'I don't know what happened to you, Pa, but you seem a changed man,' she enthused.

He didn't feel about to tell her as no doubt she would hardly believe it but he did consider hanging around afterwards to have a word with Reverend Aylward about the experience.

***

'You're not going to fall for that, are you, Eliza?' Michael said to his sister later when she called back at the house to collect her clothing to take over to the Whittle house.

'Look, Michael. I'm telling you. Pa seems different to me.'

'I don't see how that can be the case!' he said, throwing up his hands as if in disbelief. 'He's just trying to fool us all he always was a bit of a trickster.'

Eliza chewed on her lower lip. 'I don't think so. He'd cleaned himself and everything and sounded sober to me. He even made a good impression with Mr and Mrs Whittle at the blessing.'

Michael narrowed his gaze. 'What's he after? Yer in-laws got a lot of money, 'ave they?'

Eliza shook her head. 'Not as far as I know. The house they rent is bigger than this one but that's probably because there are three grown sons bringing in full wages. No, Pa wasn't after anything.'

'I'll believe it when I see it!' Michael said, spitting out the words like pips from an orange. Why couldn't her brother see what she could?

Angeline, who had been quietly pottering around in the scullery, approached. 'I think the same as Michael. You want to see how he shook me that time at my pitch, trying to get money from me to go to the pub. The booze comes before his own family.'

'See, what did I tell you!' barked Michael.

Eliza drew in a composing breath and let it out again. 'Well, I'm prepared to take a chance on him. He's still me pa, after all.'

'I hope you don't live to regret it!' Michael shouted after her as she went to climb the stairs to fetch her clothing which was already packed in the bedroom.

She turned to look at both siblings. 'Maybe it's best we don't speak about pa in this house to one another as I don't want to fall out with either of you, especially on me wedding day.'

Michael's eyes softened as he walked towards

her, taking her into his arms to give her a cuddle.

'I think you're right. If you want to see the good in Pa, then go ahead. We'll not discuss him in future. It's best all round, especially for Ma's sake.'

Eliza didn't tell him that she felt Ma was open to seeing her husband again. She didn't know why but she felt there was some sort of longing in her too, to put things right before she passed over into the next world.

***

Bertie sat in a pew at the rear of the church, clutching his flat cap in his hand. He watched Reverend Aylward collect the hymn books they'd recently used and return them to a bookstand near the piano.

He turned sharply as if catching something out of the corner of his eye and shot a confused smile in Bertie's direction.

'You're still here, Mr Barker?'

'Er, yes, Vicar. I wanted to have a word with you about something.'

The reverend walked towards where he was seated and sat down beside him. 'Now then, you're concerned about Eliza marrying so young, I assume?'

Bertie shook his head. 'No, it's not really that. I wanted to ask you all about sin...me own sin...'

'Oh, I see.' The vicar glanced at a clock on the wall. 'Well, I have a good twenty minutes or more before my housekeeper expects me for lunch, we shan't be disturbed, so go ahead...'

Bertie shook his head as tears filled his eyes. 'Most folk who speak about me will tell you what a rotter I've been. An out and out scoundrel, particularly as regards to how I've treated me family and most of all my poor wife.'

The vicar nodded but said nothing.

'Anyhow, something happened to me. I went to visit them all this morning and I'd had a few, I'm not proud of it but it was the only way I felt able to cope after what happened to me Mavis. You know she's dying?'

'Yes, I do.'

'Anyhow, it didn't go down well with me being there, asking to see her and I was put out of the house by my own children which didn't feel none too good. Even Eliza had said she didn't want me at her wedding today, and she's the only one who up until now hadn't turned against me.'

He paused for a while as if trying to find the words.

'I was walking up the alley outside the house, you know the one?'

'Yes, Christmas Alley, it's called,' said the vicar.

'I started to get the sensation there was someone following me. It fair put the wind up me I can tell you and caused the hairs on me neck to stand on end. Then I saw it, a ball of light! It mesmerised me and I fell to me knees. I can't explain quite what it was but the fear I felt was more like awe when I saw it. I asked what it wanted of me, you see there'd been a voice calling out my name, Albert. I expect this all sounds a bit daft to you?'

'No, not at all,' said the vicar with a smile, 'it's most astonishing!'

'The voice told me my family need me and it mentioned something that sounded like a verse that came from the Bible.'

The vicar angled his head to one side, curious now. 'Can you remember what that verse was?'

Bertie nodded. 'Just about. It was something about having redemption through His blood and the forgiveness of sins...'

'That is correct.'

'But what exactly is redemption, Vicar? And can I get some?' He asked with an eager expression on his face.

The vicar nodded. 'Yes. Redemption is the way to clear a debt if you like, and to be saved from sin.' He paused for a moment, fixing his gaze on the stained glass window of the nativity scene, as though trying to recall something. The baby Jesus was lying in a manger with parents, Mary and Joseph, gazing on in awe at the wonder of creation.

*'For all have sinned, and come short of the glory of God; Being justified freely by his grace through the redemption that is in Christ Jesus...*Romans chapter three, verses twenty-three and twenty-four.'

'But what must I do to have this redemption the Bible speaks of?'

'You must accept the Lord as your saviour, your guiding light...just like that light you saw in the alleyway this morning. I believe it was Himself who spoke to you to put you on the right path but it's a straight and narrow one at that.'

'Oh I do, I do accept him,' said Bertie, trembling now as he inclined his head.

Reverend Aylward touched his head with both hands and prayed over him. When he'd finished, Bertie knew for sure that he was going to leave his old life behind.

Gulping back the sobs, he asked, 'What time are the services here on Sunday, Vicar?'

'Ten o'clock in the morning and Six o'clock in the evening. But there's a service here tonight at six if you'd like to attend that too?'

Bertie nodded, not even knowing where to begin.

'Come along with me,' said the reverend smiling, 'I have a Bible in my office I can give you to read. You can read, can't you?'

'Yes, I can.' Bertie nodded.

'There's a Bible class on Monday evenings at half past seven. That would be a good start for you to learn more about the Bible.'

The tears were streaming down Bertie's face now as he profusely thanked the man. How was it that in just one day things could change so much? It was like a miracle had occurred.

Chapter Eighteen

From the corner of Mrs Featherstone's living room, Angeline watched the woman at work. The intense concentration she employed amazed her, as she furrowed her brow as the sewing needle jabbered away into the fabric being fed through the sewing machine. Today she was making several men's waistcoats for a small shop in the vicinity. Angeline had just finished work on her pitch for the time being and Tommy had taken her home with him again. The lad seemed so much happier now his friend was settled with the Sampsons. Everything appeared to be working out for the best.

'Can I make you a cup of tea?' Angeline offered the woman, rising from her chair.

Mrs Featherstone stopped working, looked up at her and smiled.

'That's very kind of you. We'll have a cup of tea together, shall we? Thomas has got to take these waistcoats over to Mrs O'Brien at the shop, so us girls will have a good natter.' Then her face took on a more serious expression. 'In fact, I have a proposition to put forward to you.'

'Oh?' Angeline wrinkled her nose.

'I'll just finish off by here, and you brew up then. There are some scones in the larder, if you arrange them on a plate and bring them with the tea, that would be lovely.'

The woman snipped a piece of stray cotton from one of the waistcoats, folded them neatly and bundled them up in brown paper tied loosely with string, and handed them to Tommy.

'There you go, son,' she said. 'You can join us later.'

'Thanks, Ma!' He beamed at her and then he winked at Angeline, whose cheeks flamed red hot.

Finally, Mrs Featherstone and Angeline were able to chat by the fireside.

'I'm thinking,' said the woman, 'I'm not getting any younger and I haven't forgotten about saying I might have a job for you here. How would you like to help me instead of selling those matches on the street corner in the cold?'

Angeline nodded eagerly. 'I'd love that,' she enthused. 'But what would you have me to do for you?'

'Oh, deliveries like Tommy's doing this morning as soon he'll be working full time to help his brothers in the fruit and veg business. So deliveries of garments to shops and houses, some of those posh residences I mentioned. Not just the clothing, but I plan on selling my cakes again, too.'

Angeline's eyes lit up as she bit into her scone, it tasted heavenly as it was spread with thick jam and cream. She savoured every morsel. 'Yes, you need to sell these!'

The woman nodded. 'Could you start as early as next week, Angeline? I know it's short notice but I need the help as soon as possible.'

'Yes, I could. Eliza is still at home during the day, working from our house as she can keep an eye on Ma, but...' she looked thoughtful for a moment.

'It's all right, dear,' said Mrs Featherstone as though pre-empting her thoughts, 'I quite understand that there are certain times of the day when you need to be home for your mother.'

She nodded. 'I can work anytime from eight o'clock up until around three or four o'clock at the latest as the children come home from school then, and Eliza goes home to George.'

'That's absolutely fine. How is your mother now?'

What could she say? That her mother was wasting away in bed, hardly speaking to anyone anymore? She hesitated for a moment.

'Not too good to be honest with you. She sleeps a lot due to the laudanum.'

Mrs Featherstone nodded with understanding. 'Maybe that's for the best though, eh?' She said, tilting her head to one side as she listened.

'Maybe, but I feel as though we don't get to talk to her much nowadays and soon she won't be here anymore,' she said, swallowing a lump in her throat that was threatening to choke her.

Quite unexpectedly, she began to shake as a bout of sobbing engulfed her.

'There, there,' Mrs Featherstone reassured. 'I didn't intend to make you cry. Here, have this,' she said, as she passed her a clean cotton handkerchief.

The woman's face looked blurred and hazy as Angeline dabbed away at her tears.

'It's all right,' she sniffed. 'It's good for me to talk about things as at home, I'm always the strong one...'

'Who does her crying in private? I'll be bound.' Mrs Featherstone smiled at her. 'Well, you've no need to be strong here, Angeline. Feel free to cry whenever you wish. Now then, let me tell you all about this job I'd like to give you while we wait for Thomas to return.'

***

It transpired that Mrs Featherstone would be employing her five days a week from a Monday to Friday. Beginning work at half past eight in the morning, when she'd be required to help the woman bake bread and cakes. Then, later on, she'd deliver those to nearby houses and shops. Afternoons would be spent helping Mrs Featherstone by clearing up from the morning's work and sometimes delivering garments around the area.

At any rate, she decided it would be far better than half freezing to death out on the street in the same place for hours on end.

***

They hadn't long finished their second cup of

tea when Tommy burst in through the front door.

'Heck, Thomas! Where's the bloomin' fire?' His mother's eyes enlarged.

'It's that m...man!' yelled Tommy, his eyes large and fearful.

'What man?' His mother frowned.

'Bobby's uncle. He's got Bobby with him.'

'Oh no!' Angeline watched as Mrs Featherstone's mouth popped open from the shock of it all. This was the worst possible news any of them could ever hear. Just when things were looking up for a change.

'Where are they now?' Angeline scowled, anger consuming her.

'Out on the street, he's dragging him along, roughly by his arm. He's got his cart of brushes with him as well. Where's our Billy?'

His mother tapped her chin as if in contemplation. 'He should be over by Church Street by now I reckon. Go and fetch him, quick as you like!'

'I'm going with him to help,' Angeline said. 'I'll leave my basket of matches here,' she said glancing at them on the table.

Mrs Featherstone nodded. 'Do take care, both of you...' was the last thing they heard as they left the place.

***

It was a good quarter of an hour before they located Billy who was not to be found on Church Street but on Fournier Street. A regular customer of his had pointed them in that direction.

When they found Billy he was in the middle of a crowd of housewives who had come out with their baskets and bowls as receptacles to purchase his wares.

'Come along and get your juicy green and red apples here!' he was shouting.

'Billy! Billy!' Tommy yelled at his brother as he waved his arms trying to catch his attention, but he was in the full swing of his sales patter oblivious to the fact how urgently he was needed. The women surrounding him surging forward to get first in the queue or else not to lose their places.

Finally, when Billy stopped his pitch and Tommy cried out, his head whipped around. He could sense something was up as he excused himself for a moment, asking a young lad standing nearby to keep an eye on his cart. Most were trusted customers though, it was just feared that someone a little more untrustworthy might pass by and see it as an opportunity to upset the apple cart as it were, but in a different sense as in the sense of robbing it blind.

The lad he put in charge often ran around the streets offering to help here and there and was rewarded with a couple of oranges or apples, or at the end of the day if bruised, a whole selection of fruit and veg.

Billy's forehead puckered into a frown as he strode quickly towards his brother. 'What's going on?'

'It's Bobby. His uncle has got hold of him!' Tommy yelled.

'But how's that, lad?'

'I saw them together not long since and came to find you. We must get him away as his uncle had his sweeping cart with him,' Tommy said, tugging at the sleeve of his brother's jacket.

***

Bertie had been thinking long and hard after yesterday's epiphany and the chat with Reverend Aylward. He'd returned to the church that evening for the service and had sat there in awe. Funny, he'd never taken much notice of church services before now but that one had been about the prodigal son and how he'd been welcomed back home by his father. He'd even slain a fatted calf for him to feast on, much to his brother, Cain's annoyance. He couldn't see his family getting a feast together for him, but he'd settle to be allowed back into the family home.

Today, he intended on finding Arnold Swindler and telling him he wouldn't be doing his dirty work not for all the tea in China, not even for a bag of gold sovereigns, he wouldn't. His idea was to try to talk some sense into the man. He knew he'd find him somewhere around the Old Nichol as that was his patch to work in as well as some of the bigger houses just outside the district.

As he walked along the street, feeling so much better as not a drop of alcohol had passed his lips since yesterday, he noticed a fracas going on.

Hey! He recognised that boy there, he was the one he'd followed the other day, deciding in the final hour to leave the lad be. He was with an older man who was shouting at Swindler and a young lad. Was that another lad he'd now got to work for him or was it young Bobby himself? And as he squinted his eyes, he noticed a familiar-looking girl there—Angeline! What on earth was she doing there? She looked as if she was about to kick old Swindler in the shin.

He strode over to them all. The whites of Swindler's eyes were now on show as if alarmed at what was going on.

'Hand the lad over to me!' The young man was saying.

'No, I will not!' yelled Swindler, 'he's me nephew!'

Meanwhile, the little lad who was in tattered, sooty clothing looked as though he was about to burst into tears at any moment.

'The lad's been sick, you old blaggard!' shouted the young man, then Bertie realised he was the young man he'd seen with the cart outside the Featherstone dwelling and he must be one of the brothers.

No one had noticed Bertie's approach as yet as they were so intent on rescuing Bobby. He rubbed his chin, wondering what to do now.

Stepping forward, he held up a vertical palm and in a loud voice said, 'Stop this at once! All of you!'

Angeline's mouth popped open in surprise at

seeing her father there.

Arnold shot Bertie a nervous smile. 'Thank goodness you're here to rescue me from this lot!' he said.

Bertie dropped his hand to his side. 'I'm not here to rescue you, Swindler. I'm here for the lad, to return him to the Sampsons.'

For a moment, Angeline looked horrified and he realised he had to reassure her. He turned his head in her direction. 'It's all right, darlin', I'm not here to hurt anyone, quite the opposite in fact. And I haven't been drinking either. Now, you and I are going to escort Bobby back to Mr and Mrs Sampson's house...'

'Don't believe him!' yelled Swindler. 'He was prepared to take a bag of sovereigns from me in payment for kidnapping the lad himself. If he'd not got himself so drunk lately, he'd have done it by now an' all.'

Bertie felt his face flush as his neck shrunk into the collar of his shirt with shame. How must he appear to everyone with his track record? 'You're right, Swindler,' he said, shaking his head. 'But I had changed my mind. I had tried to kidnap young Tommy first, with a view to him leading me to Bobby. But I just couldn't do it as I thought of my own children who I've failed. I was on my way to you today to tell you I wanted no more to do with any of it.'

Tommy looked at him and smiled. 'You're the man who saw me watching the somersaulting monkeys in the shop window, aren't you?'

He nodded in confirmation at him. 'Aye, lad.'

'It's true, he didn't lay a finger on me. We just had a chuckle at the monkeys' antics, that was all.'

Billy, who had said nothing since Bertie had spoken, nodded. 'I'm taking a chance, but I'll allow you to escort Bobby back home with your daughter as long as Tommy goes with you. I can't leave my pitch for much longer as I've got a young lad watching the cart for me and a large crowd of housewives waiting to be served.'

'Yes, that will be fine and most understandable,' said Bertie, then turning towards Swindler he said, 'Leave him go, Arnold. It's for the best. The lad has been sick lately and he's got a good home to go to. It's not acceptable using climbing lads or lasses these days and it's against the law. You wouldn't want the law to collar you now, would you?'

Bertie said his piece in such a way that Swindler was in no doubt if he carried on what he was doing, then he'd be reported to the police, and as he was often on the wrong side of the law anyhow regarding several thefts at the big houses, then there was a good chance he'd receive a hefty prison sentence for his time and trouble.

Reluctantly, Swindler released Bobby from his grasp and nodded. Then without further ado, and without uttering a single word, he turned and walked away, pushing his cart into the distance.

Angeline surged forward and took the trembling Bobby into her arms as he wept tears of relief at being rescued in her comforting embrace.

Chapter Nineteen

Angeline glanced hesitantly at her father as they walked along the street, with Tommy and Bobby in tow. It was as if Tommy was taking no chances as far as his mate was concerned, the way he escorted him with a reassuring arm around the lad's shoulders. Angeline, herself, couldn't fully trust Pa until she'd seen Bobby safely delivered to his charges. Every time she looked at her father, she thought he seemed like a different person, more mellow somehow. Yet, could someone change that much? Had he received a blow to the head that might have somehow changed his personality? After all, he'd been in trouble in the past with gambling debts and various creditors.

As they continued to walk with extreme purpose towards home, she noticed how her father kept pausing and turning around every so often to check Bobby was all right. The boy appeared happy now he was on his way back to the shop and would be safe and secure with the Sampsons.

Pa began to relate tales of his boyhood in the area, Tommy and Bobby listening with avid interest.

'There's me old auntie's house over there!' Pa pointed a finger. 'She didn't have much but we always had the best Christmases at her gaff. And everyone got a warm welcome no matter what time of the year it was.'

'There's the old boneyard there!' He pointed in another direction. 'Old Mr Hopson was one of the grave diggers there, until he could dig them graves no longer. I used to help him for a couple of pennies, that was when I was about your age, lads.'

A shiver coursed Angeline's spine at the mention of the graveyard. She never knew about her father's auntie or old Hopson as he'd never told her those stories before.

There seemed to be a lightness in his step as though he were enjoying life as he related those tales to them all. What on earth had happened to cause that?

When they drew up near the shop, Bobby began to beam from ear to ear and then he started to weep, but those were joyful tears of relief at going back home to his loving guardians.

'I'll just step inside with the lad and explain what's happened today,' Pa said. 'You pair wait outside and if you behave yourselves, I might fetch you some Bentley's chocolate drops.'

Tommy nodded with a big smile on his face, Angeline, though, narrowed her gaze. This all seemed to be too good to be true as though she were in a dream where Pa had been replaced by the father she'd always longed for.

When her father had escorted Bobby inside and they heard the bell above the door tinkle, Tommy turned to her and said, 'What's the matter with you? Aren't you pleased for Bobby?'

'Yes, of course I am. It's my Pa. He's acting sort of odd. He's not usually this kind and amusing.'

Tommy shrugged. 'I don't know what to think, to be honest, as I don't know him like you do. But one thing's for certain, he helped to rescue Bobby today. Bobby's uncle took notice of what he said. I don't think he would have listened like that to Billy. He'd 'ave had to resort to fisticuffs to rescue him!' He held up both fists in a boxing stance which caused Angeline to giggle, breaking the feeling of fear she had.

'I suppose you're right, Tommy. It's the first good thing I've seen my Pa do in ever such a long time...' she paused to think for a moment, 'and he did turn up at the church for the wedding blessing, Eliza told me.'

Tommy grinned. 'There you go then! Everyone deserves a second chance.'

***

When Tommy had finally left them to head off back home, Angeline looked at her father and said, 'Pa, what's happened to you?'

He smiled and nodded at her. 'I can't explain it properly to you as you'd never believe me...'

'Please tell me,' she urged, 'as I just don't understand.'

'Very well,' he paused for a moment at the end

of the road, before beginning to speak, confusion written over his face. 'It was on that morning of Eliza's wedding when I was shown the door.'

Her face suffused with heat, as she was one of those to show him the door and when she thought back on it, none of them had wanted to listen to what he'd had to say.

'I'm sorry Pa, but we didn't want you ruining things for Eliza that morning.'

'Yes, I realise that now, but I didn't at the time. So, I left there all bewildered but then the strangest thing happened...' Pa's face took on almost an ethereal expression, not one Angeline had ever seen previously.

'Tell me about it, Pa. I won't think it's silly. I promise.' She looked on with longing and anticipation as the change in him wasn't anything she'd ever witnessed before.

Pa shook his head, almost as if to shake himself out of his reverie.

'I had the sense of someone following after me. I kept turning my head to look behind me, but there was no one there.' He took a deep composing breath and let it out again, 'but then I saw it!'

'What Pa? What did you see?' Angeline's eyes grew large.

'A glowing ball of light...' Pa's face illuminated and as he spoke of it, his eyes shone as though he were in absolute awe by the memory of the whole experience.

A shiver ran the length of Angeline's spine as a

recent memory returned to her as hadn't she and Eliza seen the same thing? And in Christmas Alley, too. Though she thought it had been because she was tired and cold and maybe she'd imagined it.

She opened her mouth and closed it again.

'What's the matter?' said her father as he looked into her eyes. 'You look like you've seen a ghost? I'm not scaring you, am I, dear girl?'

'Oh, no. Not at all, Pa. It's just something strange happened to me and Eliza on Christmas Eve and in the alleyway too.'

'Then it can't be my imagination playing tricks. Someone spoke to me,' he said excitedly. 'I was in awe, is all I can say and I dropped to my knees. It was almost as if the radiance was blinding me, to begin with. I could barely look at the light to start with, it took some time for me to become accustomed to it. But I realised somehow this was a greater power than myself at work.'

'What did the voice say?'

'It or he or she spoke of redemption. I told the vicar about what happened yesterday and we spoke of how I can redeem myself, it's not too late. I've started to go to church an' all.'

Angeline gulped in disbelief. Pa as a churchgoer? His church up until now had been the pub and not just drinking the ale either, he'd been caught up in a whirlwind of illegal gambling and mixing with nefarious sorts. Now he appeared to want to turn his back on all of that. Was it just an act for her benefit? But no, it couldn't be as she'd never told him about what she'd seen in that alleyway before now.

'Pa,' she said softly, 'I saw the ball of light too.'

He lifted his eyebrows. 'You did? When was that?'

'It was the afternoon when we'd all gone Carol singing. I went to see Mrs Sampson and she gave me this beautiful angel doll but me and Eliza, well...' she hesitated as if trying to choose her words carefully, but in the end decided to be blunt. 'We decided to sell the doll, you see. After you took the package of meat and poultry Mr Styles had given us to eat over Christmas.'

She watched as her father's face flushed crimson and he stood there as if in disbelief at what she was telling him. Then he shook his head.

'I am so very sorry,' he said. 'It shouldn't have come to that—you all having to do without for me to sell off that parcel of meat from the butcher. So what happened to the doll?'

'In the end, I decided to pawn it to Mr Goodman and he thought it might be one of those expensive dolls that people collect, but it wasn't. He took pity on me and returned it and said I didn't need to give back the money he'd given me. So I still have the doll.'

'How kind was that,' said Pa. 'I'm that ashamed of myself I am that I left you all in dire straits like that. It's almost as though I was a different person then, even though it wasn't all that long ago.'

She nodded. 'Anyhow, it was while Eliza had

been teasing me while we were walking down the alleyway, we saw the ball of light. It seemed to be directing us home as Ma needed us.'

Her father now had tears in his eyes. 'Well, she would have after what I put her through over Christmas.'

'Is it really over now between you and that barmaid?'

'Aye, it is. Once I realised how ill your mother was, I put a stop to it. I moved out of her place and got myself a rented room over the pub. I've now put pay to all my shenanigans.'

Angeline looked at her father and could see there was genuine remorse on his face and probably in his heart.

'I'll take you to see Ma, then,' she said, smiling.

***

Pa hesitated outside the door of their house. Looking up at it, he wiped away a tear with the sleeve of his jacket.

'Are you sure Michael won't be there?' he asked, tentatively 'I wouldn't want to upset him.'

Angeline smiled. 'No, he told me he has lots of extra deliveries this afternoon as one of the new lads taken on by Mr Styles has come down with a sickness, so he's rushed off his feet.'

She pushed open the door as Eliza looked up from a mountain of matchboxes. She appeared about to say something to her sister, and then spotting their father, she was on her feet and rushed towards him with her arms open wide.

'Oh Pa,' she said hugging him, 'you've come to see us!'

'Yes,' he nodded, 'though I know if Michael was here, I'd be put on my way.'

'I hope he'll come around soon,' said Angeline as she removed her shawl and went to put the kettle on to boil. It was good to have Pa in the home again, especially as he appeared to be making such an effort.

Eliza had almost finished assembling her matchboxes for the day, so she cleared the pile away into a box which would be collected later. Now the table was clear for them to take a cup of tea together and there was some of Mrs Featherstone's cake left over for them to enjoy.

When Pa had eaten his fill and carried on sipping his cup of tea, now everyone was on their second cup, he looked intently at both daughters with love in his eyes.

He stretched his hands out across the table, one in each direction, one to hold Eliza's and the other to take hold of Angeline's.

'I never thought I'd ever do this again,' he said as he inclined his head and his sobs overtook him. 'I've been a very foolish man...'

'Aw, Pa,' said Eliza, now on her knees beside him. 'I never gave up on you, that's why I wanted you at my wedding and asked your permission to marry George. And I think,' she said, glancing across at her sister, 'neither did Angeline.'

It was partly true, Angeline thought. Although

he'd shaken the living daylights out of her, she had once remembered him as a good father before the drink and his wanton ways had taken hold. Now, she too, stood and moved closer to Pa, wrapping her arms around his neck and openly sobbing with him.

And then, the door burst open, as Michael walked in.

'What a pretty scene we have here!' he barked, angrily.

'Please sit and listen,' said Eliza, rising to her feet. 'Pa has changed, he wants to make amends to us all.'

'I've heard it all before,' he glared at his father, 'and quite honestly, I'll have to see it for myself before I believe any of it!'

Angeline walked towards Michael. 'Please, do this for us, for Ma. She's not got long left and she'd hate to think now she's leaving this world that there'd be no parent left for us.'

Michael shook his head, but he took a seat at the table anyhow. 'I'm only doing this for Ma's sake,' he said.

Eliza nodded. 'How come you're back so soon? We thought you were working overtime because of that lad going off sick?'

'I am still working late, but Mr Styles sent me home for a break before I take out the orders. I thought I'd call in for a cuppa, not realising of course that *he'd* be here!'

'Then a cuppa you shall have,' said Angeline. She

threw a clean cloth over the bare table and went off to boil the kettle again.

For an awkward few minutes, Pa and Michael spoke through Eliza as the tea was brewed, but then, when Angeline joined them all with a fresh pot and a sandwich she'd prepared for her brother, the awkwardness ebbed away and finally Pa and Michael were talking properly to one another once again.

When Michael had finished eating, he looked at his father and asked, 'So, you actually saw the light?'

'Yes, I did.' Nodded Pa. 'I can't explain it to you properly but I felt a very loving presence.'

'Are you sure it weren't the drink?' Michael chuckled.

'Yes. I know it was real.'

'We saw it too, Michael, me and Eliza on Christmas Eve.'

'I thought I was dreaming at first,' said Eliza, 'it didn't last for long and didn't seem as powerful as what happened to Pa. But it happened.'

'So, I've started going to church,' said Pa. 'And I'd like you kids to come with me this Sunday.'

Angeline nodded eagerly though both Eliza and Michael were slow to answer.

'Please,' said Pa. 'I know you have George to see to and he'll not be working that day, so bring him along. And you, Michael, I know you've worked hard all week but we can go as a family and pray for your mother.'

Michael swallowed hard as Angeline noticed tears in her brother's eyes, it was the first time she'd seen those in all the time Ma had been ill. Michael was just about to say something when the door burst open as Sammy and Joanna came rushing in, school having finished for the day. It was the first time they'd been allowed to walk home without being accompanied by an older sibling.

'Pa!' they shouted in unison and both came hurtling over to the table to hug him. Out of all Pa's offspring, this pair were the most accepting of him, even when he was in the dog house. And they were the two who needed their father the most at their young ages.

'Hello, you two!' he said, with an arm around each as they stood on either side of the chair. 'How did school go today?'

'Mrs Greening gave us homework!' said Sammy as though quite proud of it.

'And what sort of homework did she give you?'

'We have to find out where our grandparents lived and what they did!' Joanna enthused.

'Oh that's easy,' chuckled Pa. 'My father, Grandpa Benjamin Barker, was a dockworker and my mother, Grandma Millicent, whose surname was Crowther before she married, was a seamstress. They lived in the east end of London not too far from here.'

'What about Ma's mother and father?' asked Joanna.

'Ah, now, they were an interesting couple,' Pa said thoughtfully. 'Grandma Ivy O'Leary, O'Leary was her maiden name you see, was from Southern Ireland. She loved embroidery and ended up embroidering a lovely linen tablecloth as a wedding present.'

'I know it!' yelled Joanna suddenly. 'Ma put it on the table for Christmas day.'

'Did she now?' Pa had a wistful look in his eyes and Angeline guessed it was because, for the first time ever, he hadn't been a part of Christmas day celebrations with his family. 'Well, Grandpa Manning, was an office clerk...' he let out a long breath. 'Unfortunately, all your grandparents are no longer with us. I lost my parents when I was quite young, you see.'

For the first time, Angeline noticed a look of compassion in her brother's eyes as he listened intently now to Pa's tales of when he was a young lad. It was as if they were all viewing their father properly for the very first time.

When Pa had finished speaking, Angeline glanced up at the ceiling. 'I'd better take a cup of tea up to Ma,' she said.

'I'd like to do that, if I may?' Pa asked, and looking particularly at Michael, Michael nodded in agreement.

It would probably take some time for everyone to come around to Pa wanting to be involved in their lives again, particularly Ma's, but inroads had been made and now it was time for reconciliation and as Pa had put it, his redemption.

Chapter Twenty

Angeline packed a selection of Mrs Featherstone's iced buns, fondant fancies and currant buns, into the large wicker basket that the woman had provided, covering it with a clean tray cloth.

'Now then,' said Mrs Featherstone with a big beaming smile on her face. 'These are the first orders of the day. You're to call with them to a little tea shop called, "The Silver Kettle". I've written the address down and directions for you.' She handed over a folded slip of paper and Angeline nodded at her, all the while marvelling that she no longer had to stand on street corners plying her wares as Mrs Featherstone had done her homework, drumming up custom in the area.

The woman was already well known and her good reputation went before her, plus, people remembered her fondly from when she'd previously sold her cakes years since.

'Am I to be paid when I drop them off at the tea shop?' Angeline asked anxiously, not wanting to let the woman down.

'No, not in this instance. Mrs Bell, the lady who owns it, has already paid me in advance. So, get those delivered on time and we'll really be in business as then she'll want to order more. She used to bake herself for the shop but as she explained to me, her arthritis in her fingers makes it a long and difficult task these days.'

'She'll be glad of the help, then!' Angeline smiled.

'That she will.' Mrs Featherstone winked at her.

'What about the other customers?' Angeline asked as she eyed up the various batches of cakes cooling on wire trays on the counter.

'Well, those will be different. Now, I know you must be a good salesgirl as you often manage to sell all your matches, Angeline. So I'm relying on you to go door-to-door to some of the shops and offices and ask if anyone would like to purchase a penny bun. Hopefully, if they buy today, you can sell again tomorrow to them. Today will be hardest though as no one will know you as yet, but just mention my name, and most know me around here.' She held the open palm of her hand to her chest and let out a small sigh.

Angeline realised this was a big day for the woman. It was a big day for Tommy too as he was joining his brothers in the coster business and would be helping Billy on the cart to start off, with a view to him maybe having a cart himself someday to drum up some extra business.

Before leaving, there was one question on Angeline's lips that she was keen to know the answer to. 'How is Bobby doing back with Mr and Mrs Sampson?' she enquired.

Mrs Featherstone smiled. 'Aw, he's doing well bless him. I called into the shop just yesterday as Tommy wanted to see him. He seems none the worse for his recent ordeal though Mrs Sampson said they were fraught with anxiety when he was snatched like that. And they feared they'd never see him again.'

Angeline could well imagine. Maybe if Pa hadn't happened to come along at such a time, the lad might never have been seen by any of them again as his uncle could well have started him climbing chimneys elsewhere.

'That's good, he's back where he belongs.'

'That uncle of his deserves a good horsewhipping, Billy told me all about him.'

'I agree, but I think he'll listen to my father now.'

'I hope so, Angeline. I sincerely hope so. He's such a fragile-looking child. That time I was caring for him, I feared he wouldn't make it but he must be strong despite his appearance, I suppose.'

Angeline guessed the woman was right.

***

The Silver Kettle Tea Shop was located on the main high street, nestled in between a lady's clothing shop and a tobacconist. Angeline paused to admire the beautiful peacock-coloured gown in the window of the shop next door. She blew out a hard breath. Imagine having the money to be able to afford that.

'I'll buy you something like that one day...'

She turned around to see Pa stood behind her

with a big smile on his face.

'Pa, what are you doing here?' She blinked.

'I'm looking for a job. The vicar gave me a couple of addresses to enquire at.' He held up a piece of paper in his hand.

'As a chimney sweep?' She frowned as she considered Bobby's recent ordeal, it had coloured her views of sweeps in general for the present.

'No, not as one of those. It's too demanding a job for me and to be truthful, I don't wish to return to it.'

'Then what sort of a job, Pa?'

'Well, I can turn my hand to a lot of different things, when I'm not too idle I suppose,' he chuckled. 'But one of the jobs on here is to work at a new coffee tavern that's being set up to keep people on the straight and narrow.'

Angeline tilted her head to one side. What on earth did Pa mean by that?

'I can see I've got you puzzled. It's set up by the Temperance Movement which I've joined. It's to help people keep off the alcohol and for them to drink other things instead. I think as well as coffee they'll provide other drinks like hot chocolate and ginger beer, lemonade, that sort of thing. They might even hold some kind of meetings there.'

She nodded her approval at him. 'I hope you're lucky then. What's the other job?'

'A lady living in one of the big houses called, Mrs Billington, is looking for a handyman, I used to sweep her chimneys for her. She's seeking someone who's a jack of all trades by all accounts.'

'Which would you prefer out of the two, Pa?'

'I don't much mind, to be honest with you as long as I get myself a job.'

Angeline thought for a moment. 'When you get yourself a job, will you be moving back in with us?'

Pa shrugged his shoulders. 'I'm not too sure as yet. Now your mother is used to me calling in to see her, I don't want to chance my arm, but I'll know when and if the time is right. Meanwhile, I suppose I better look for different digs though as being above a barroom has its own temptations.'

Angeline could well imagine it might be torture for her father to even get the merest sniff of alcohol. Maybe that's why he wanted to keep himself busy and well away from the place.

He leant down to peck a kiss on her cheek. 'Anyhow, I'd best be going,' he said with a forced cheerfulness.

'Good luck, Pa,' she smiled at him.

'And the same to you on the first day of your new job with Mrs Featherstone, darlin'!'

Then he turned and walked away from her. Seeing him like that quite out of the blue had tugged at her heartstrings as she wondered if they'd all be a family again?

***

The tea shop was quite cheery inside with its tables adorned with blue and white gingham tablecloths and small flower arrangements as a centrepiece at each one. The wide windows were adorned with fancy lace curtains with scalloped edges. The place smelled of vanilla and cinnamon with a faint waft of coffee going on somewhere. Although it was a tea room it was quite fashionable to have a cup of coffee these days. Angeline loved a cup whenever she could get one, which wasn't all that often. But Mrs Sampson had given her one now and again and so had Mrs Featherstone. At home, they mostly made do with cups of tea and if very hard up, they dried out the leaves and reused them.

'Can I help you, miss?' A young waitress who was around Eliza's age asked. She stood near the door as though greeting those who entered and most probably showing them to a table.

'I'm here to see, Mrs Bell,' Angeline said, her eyes still taking in the room and everything about it enchanted her. She hoped one day she might own a tea room such as this.

The girl smiled at her. 'I'm her daughter, Kate. I'll go and fetch her,' she said, glancing at Angeline's wicker basket which she still carried over the crook of her arm. 'She's expecting you if you're the girl with the cakes?'

Angeline nodded enthusiastically. 'Yes, I've got her order from Mrs Featherstone. I'm Angeline Barker.'

The girl nodded at her. 'I shan't be a tick.'

Angeline stood waiting patiently as she watched an elderly couple in the corner share a pot of what looked like coffee together, along with a plate of fancies. Maybe it was their morning ritual to come to The Silver Kettle or maybe it was the lady's birthday. Angeline liked making up stories in her head about folk she didn't know, it was a way of amusing herself.

Ma had often said she had a vivid imagination, unlike Eliza who seemed to have little imagination at all and who got bored very easily.

Presently, a middle-aged woman dressed in a long dark blue dress with lace collar and cuffs came striding towards her. She seemed a hasty sort to Angeline.

'Ah, Miss Barker,' she said in a clipped tone of voice, extending her gnarled-looking hand for a shake, which Angeline guessed were those arthritic fingers Mrs Featherstone had mentioned. This seemed most unusual to Angeline, it was only gentlemen she'd ever seen do such a thing but she allowed the woman to take her hand and give it a firm shake.

'Here are the iced buns, fondant fancies and currant buns you ordered, Mrs Bell,' Angeline said, removing the tray cloth from the basket for the woman's approval.

Mrs Bell peered inside and nodded. 'They all look good to me. I've dealt with Mrs Featherstone before now, when I first opened this place and I know they'll be up to their usual standard.' She glanced at her daughter who'd been standing nearby the whole time as though out of curiosity. 'Kate, take this basket through to the kitchen and unpack those cakes and put them under the glass domes for later. Then return the basket to ...er, sorry I didn't catch your name?'

The woman hadn't caught her name as she hadn't given it to her but she had to the waitress.

'Angeline Barker,' Kate said smiling, and then she winked at Angeline.

'That's a lovely name, Angeline. Now go and sit at one of those tables and I'll fetch you something for your trouble today. What would you like?'

Angeline didn't need to be asked twice as she knew what she desired the most. 'A cup of coffee, please?'

Mrs Bell quirked an eyebrow. 'Well, of all the things you might have had here, eclairs and fancy sandwiches, you would like a cup of coffee. Are you sure?'

'Yes, please,' Angeline nodded.

'How very grown up of you!' The woman chuckled. 'Then a cup of coffee you shall have, my girl!'

The truth of it was that by the end of the day, Mrs Featherstone would have offered her so many of her cakes, that she'd feel right stuffed. The woman seemed to offer those that had either got overbaked or were too small to sell or else had got dropped on the floor or whatever. So a cup of coffee would do just nicely. She had to return to the woman's house later with her empty basket to fill up with buns, to try selling around the shops, so she was thankful for the opportunity to rest her weary legs as she'd been standing helping in the kitchen for the past couple of hours and her legs ached something rotten.

Kate returned her empty basket complete with tray cloth and showed her to a window seat where she was able to watch the activity going on outside. Then Mrs Bell arrived with a silver tray containing an earthenware coffee pot, complete with a matching cup and saucer, milk jug and a small pot with some brown granules inside.

Angeline wrinkled her nose. What was inside that? The question was on the tip of her tongue but then the woman said, 'Don't worry none, dear. It's demerara sugar that goes so well with coffee.'

Angeline nodded at her and when the woman departed, she tried a little on her finger. The brown crystals seemed bigger than white sugar crystals, and tasting a little on the tip of her tongue, it seemed a little crunchy, tasting of caramel and toffee. It met with her approval, so she spooned some into her coffee cup, and stirring well, took a sip. Mrs Bell was right, it did go very well with the coffee.

She sat and stared out of the window, enjoying her cup of coffee and reflecting on Pa and his recently reformed behaviour.

A little voice inside her gave her a nudge as it questioned would this new reformed version of her father last? And would he live up to his promises?

***

It was a busy first day for Angeline, she was run off her feet after that cup of coffee, so it was good she'd had a break. As she was leaving the tea room, she thanked Mrs Bell. The woman had smiled at her and said it had been good doing business.

Then Angeline returned to see Mrs Featherstone to collect the next batch of cakes and buns. The woman had suggested she allow people to sample the wares first before buying.

After visiting several shops and a couple of offices, the staff of one premise in particular seemed most keen. That was the offices owned by Harding, Harding and Fisher which was a firm of solicitors. It was a long wait as Angeline sat on a hardbacked leather chair watching as various people visited rooms behind thick wood-panelled doors. She wondered what they were discussing and why, in some cases, they were taking so long to emerge. The people who waited were rewarded for their patience when their names were called out by the firm's secretary who showed them to the room where their appointment was to be held. The smartly dressed, elegant secretary, finally approached Angeline with a smile on her face to inform her that the staff who worked there would be most interested in making regular orders if a selection of sandwiches could be provided too.

For a moment, Angeline had been speechless as she didn't know how to answer on behalf of Mrs Featherstone, but then she decided to use sound judgement else she might lose the woman the order. Replying in the affirmative, she nodded and thought if supplying sandwiches brought in more business then that had to be a good thing.

Mrs Featherstone had been more than happy when she'd related the news to her and had told her to run back over to the office and take their orders for that very same day.

Later, there were several packages of clothing for her to deliver to a gentleman's outfitters. One was a package of men's waistcoats and the other, several twill shirts. By the afternoon she was all but worn out, but happy. And now there was the journey back home as her legs ached.

Pa had called to Mrs Featherstone's to walk her back home and the woman had presented him with a currant bun and a cup of tea, which he was grateful for.

The woman took a seat by the fireside opposite him and the pair chatted away merrily, as though they were old friends, which surprised Angeline as she couldn't have seen that happening even just a couple of months ago.

On the journey home, Angeline looked at her father, 'How did the interviews go today, Pa?'

She watched as he forced a smile. 'Not so bad though...' he paused for a moment as if trying to choose his words carefully, 'I don't think either will end up hiring me.'

'Why do you say that?' she said, linking arms with her father.

''Cos of my reputation, see. I know someone

working at the coffee tavern recognised me and I saw her nudge the woman behind the counter when I came in.' He shook his head. 'It's my own fault.'

'And the lady at the big house, Mrs Billington?'

'I don't know about her either. She was nice enough as she recognised me even though I haven't been there to sweep her chimneys in years, but there was a man there also waiting to be interviewed and he was half my age and looked very spruced up. If I was that lady, I'd have hired him.'

'You never know though, Pa. You might be lucky as perhaps that lady would prefer someone more mature and don't forget that old saying, "Never judge a book by its cover!"'

He shrugged his shoulders. 'We'll see.'

'Did she take your address?'

He nodded. 'Yes, she did.'

'Well there you are then, that's got to be a hopeful sign. If she wasn't interested, I doubt she would do that.'

'Yes, maybe you're right, my little angel.' A slow smile spread across her father's lips. 'Now then, I'll walk you home and call in to see your mother at the same time.'

She nodded her approval at him. It was so good to have Pa back in her life and she didn't want anything to come between them ever again as a family.

Chapter Twenty One

As they both entered the house, Angeline realised something wasn't right, she had a sense of foreboding. There was no sign of Eliza sitting at the table assembling her matchboxes. The house itself seemed unnaturally quiet. But it wasn't peaceful by any means, there was an uneasy feeling. She glanced at her father who must have been sensing it too as his eyes enlarged and he made for the stairs.

Not Ma, oh no not, Ma!

As he turned the knob and slowly eased open the bedroom door, Angeline's body convulsed as she saw the slight form of her mother lying there, eyes wide open, wax-like in the bed with Eliza kneeling beside her, holding Ma's hand as tears spilt down her cheeks.

Looking up at them, her bottom lip quivered as she said, 'Ma's gone, she's really gone. It was no use even fetching the doctor. I took her a cup of tea earlier and she seemed to have perked up a little. Then I left to do me work and when I called up again an hour later, she was gone, all cold, but it seemed peaceful.'

Pa nodded, and then he placed his hand over his

wife's eyes to close her eyelids. Approaching Eliza, he helped her to her feet and hugged her. 'There was no more you could do, dear girl,' he said softly. 'Now go on downstairs with your sister and have a cup of tea together. I'll join you later but right now, if you don't mind, I need to have some time alone with your mother.'

Both girls nodded and left the room, Angeline trying to take it all in. Of course, they knew Ma was dying, the doctor had been very frank with them about that but Ma seemed to have perked up recently since Pa had been coming to see her again. Oh, what a pity he'd left them all like that at Christmas to have blotted his copybook. But then again, he was always blotting it. Except for now. Now Pa had turned a page and arrived on a clean sheet. He was being a proper father to them at long last.

Angeline's thoughts turned to Michael. 'I better go and tell our Michael,' she said looking at Eliza but seeing the state of the girl, she considered what was best to do in the circumstances—it wouldn't hurt Michael to wait a few more minutes to be told of something that would affect the rest of his life.

'I'll make us a cup of tea and then I'll go over to the shop to ask if he may be allowed home for an hour or so. We can tell Sammy and Joanna later when they return from school, it serves no purpose to upset them right now.'

Eliza nodded with a catatonic stare. It was

hardest on her sister as in recent weeks she was the one who had spent most time with their mother as she worked from home.

Truth be told though, it would be hard on them all, especially the one who felt the most guilt of all.

***

The day of the funeral was a stark contrast to how Angeline felt. Outside, for the first time in a long while, there were blue skies penetrated by a soft pale yellow winter sun. How could it be such a beautiful day when she felt so empty and hollow inside? As though nothing or no one mattered to her any more. She was just going through the motions.

Mrs Featherstone had kindly told her not to arrive to help out for the next few days, following her mother's death. The woman had said she'd manage as Thomas could pop back from the coster round from time to time to help with any deliveries. Mr Styles had given Michael the rest of his shift off when he'd been told of his mother's death and he was being allowed the day of the funeral and the following day off too. People had been most understanding.

Pa hadn't been offered either job in the end, and in a way, he said he was thankful for small mercies as he didn't feel he'd cope very well right now and wanted to support his family.

He had somehow managed to scrape together the money for a decent funeral for his wife. Angeline wondered how he'd done so but Michael reckoned he must have sold his old chimney sweeping round on to someone, complete with the necessary tools and cart. But, Angeline doubted all the money came from that.

Even so, there wasn't enough money for a full horse-drawn hearse, those with the black plumage and blinkers. Folk like them made do with some sort of cart either from the undertaker or one they provided themselves. But in this instance, this was the funeral director's horse and cart with the family procession walking the short distance behind as they headed towards the church where the Reverend Aylward would conduct the service. Some of Ma's old friends from the match factory turned out, those that had either finished there or were on a later shift. They stood solemn in their dark attire, with shawls around their heads and shoulders, marching behind the cart as their clogs rhythmically hit the pavements.

Angeline realised that those women and girls must have been wondering if any of them, or anyone they knew who worked at the factory, could be next. It was well known now about that phossy jaw thing and the other diseases they could succumb to from working with the white powder. Yet the bosses did nothing about it.

Eliza had been particularly bitter about it all when Ma passed away and swore she'd never make another matchbox ever again, and was glad Angeline had stopped selling matches on street corners too. Angeline guessed that it wasn't just that that caused her sister's upset, it was because while she was busy assembling those matchboxes that day, Ma had slipped away. Maybe there was some guilt there somewhere. And that was perfectly understandable but as Pa had told them both, they had done no wrong whatsoever, they'd both been there for their mother when she needed them most, which was something he hadn't been until it was far too late.

'*The Lord giveth and the Lord taketh away...*' Reverend Aylward was saying as their mother's coffin was being lowered into the ground as the chief mourners surrounded the graveside.

Angeline swallowed hard as she gripped Pa's hand. He hadn't said much this morning, he'd been particularly quiet. Eliza stood with Sammy and Joanna holding her hand on each side and behind those, stood Michael. He'd been unable to cry since hearing of their mother's death, preferring instead, to come home from work and after attempting to eat his evening meal, then saying "Good Night" to them all, and climbing into bed. Sometimes he even went to bed just after Sammy and Joanna, which was virtually unknown as Michael was renowned for being a night owl, despite rising early mornings for work at the shop.

Angeline didn't know who to be more concerned about: Pa, Eliza or Michael. Strangely enough, she wasn't so concerned about the two little ones as they seemed accepting of the situation. After all, to them, Ma was going to heaven and they'd get to see her again at some time.

A tear trickled down Angeline's cheek as she gazed up at the yew trees surrounding the graveyard. The snow on them was thawing, and now they appeared to be crying too as droplets of melting snow splashed occasionally from their branches. She remembered Ma once telling her that yew trees symbolised the journey of the soul from this life to the next. Well, she hoped that was true and Ma's journey would be a good one.

Pa had been particularly quiet so far, and his hand now felt like a block of ice. She looked up at him with blurred vision and could see the pain etched on his face, the remorse evident to see, today of all days. What really mattered was he had returned to their mother in the end and been there when she most needed him even if he hadn't moved back into the home. It would be Pa taking her the first cup of tea of the day, Pa boiling water to fill the stone hot water bottle to warm her up, Pa even brushing her hair and washing her face. It had been a joy to see her father care so deeply for Ma in the end. And she knew how desperately sorry he was, so remorseful for all he'd put them through, particularly his dear Mavis.

Reverend Aylward held the long handle of a small rectangular wooden box containing earth, which he offered around. The chief mourners took a handful each, sprinkling it on top of Ma's coffin, which was now lowered six feet beneath the ground.

Angeline glanced to her right to see Eliza comforting the two little ones with George beside her. He was going to make her sister a good husband that was for sure.

Michael was now standing alongside a well-dressed gentleman who wore a black top hat, there was something familiar about him but for the moment she couldn't quite place him. There was no time to ponder any further as now the reverend was saying the committal prayer.

O God,
by whose mercy the faithful departed find rest,
bless this grave,
and send your holy angel to watch over it.
As we bury here the body of our sister,
deliver her soul from every bond of sin,
that she may rejoice in you with your saints for ever.
We ask this through Christ our Lord.
Amen.

It now all seemed so final. So ultimate. So absolute.

Glancing over her shoulder, Angeline noticed two men casually dressed, well away from all the other mourners. Their backs were propped up against the wall. By the side of them were two shovels. She gulped as she realised those were a pair of gravediggers ready to fill in the grave. And now she felt like throwing herself into that open grave alongside her mother as she'd never get that near her ever again, at least not in this world.

As though noticing her distress, her father, who appeared to have shaken himself out of his reverie, drew her close to him and hugged her tightly to his chest.

'It's all right, Angeline. Let it go...'

She cried like she'd never cried before as shuddering sobs engulfed her entire being and when her crying spell was over, she noticed everyone had departed but the vicar, the man in the top hat and the pair of gravediggers.

That was odd, why was the man in the top hat hanging around? The vicar and the gravediggers being there was understandable, but his presence puzzled her.

As if reading her thoughts, Pa tilted Angeline's chin with his thumb and forefinger as he softly said, 'That's Mr Styles the butcher over there. He kindly offered his coach to take us back to the house. Michael has said he'll walk back home with the kids and George and Eliza are doing the same. So come on, gal, you and I shall ride in style for once in our lives.'

Angeline couldn't believe the kindness of the man, but then again, maybe she could as hadn't he gifted them all a package of meat over Christmas? And he was a good employer to Michael who spoke highly of him. Maybe it was Mr Styles who had helped pay something towards Ma's funeral?

As they sat in Mr Style's coach with the man, Angeline imagined it was all a dream, and when they'd return home, Ma would be still there, coughing upstairs in her bedroom while everyone fussed over her.

If only that were the case as she'd give anything to have her mother back even if it was for just one day, but then she reminded herself, if that were to happen, it would be one more day for her mother to suffer and she just did not want that at all.

Chapter Twenty two

It had been suggested by Mr Styles that Pa hold the funeral tea at a local pub, but Pa had told Michael he didn't want that at all as there'd be too much temptation for him, and besides, such a large venue wasn't warranted as only close family members, one or two of Ma's friends and the reverend, had been invited back afterwards to the family home. So instead, the man had given Michael a large cooked ham they could use and his wife had prepared some sandwiches while Mrs Featherstone had baked a rich fruit cake.

Angeline had watched her father, ever the good host, mingling with the guests, forcing a smile or two. But she realised that wasn't Pa's real smile. His real smile lit up his eyes when he spoke. His voice sounded tinged with sadness and regret. The truth was she was extremely concerned about him. So later, when all the guests had departed, she took Eliza and Michael to one side and asked them how they felt about their father moving back into the house.

Eliza had been happy about it and although Michael was hesitant at first, he finally agreed to the proposal and Angeline was able to release a long slow breath at the relief of it all.

Pa had sobbed his heart out when his three elder children had sat him down and put the idea to him. He'd been sitting in his favourite armchair at the time and he put his head in his hands as he wept.

'It's not what I deserve,' he said, dropping his hands to his sides and looking up at them. 'After the way I've treated you all, particularly your dear mother.'

Angeline didn't know what to say to that so she exchanged glances with Eliza.

But thankfully, Michael stepped in. 'Well, the main thing is you've been making amends lately, Pa. We've all seen a big change in you, and...' he paused for a moment, 'we think it's what Ma would want.'

Their father's eyes were glassy and he nodded at them. 'I thank you all for your forgiveness, all three of you. But I wish your mother had forgiven me.'

'Oh, she did, Pa.' Eliza smiled at him, taking a seat on the arm of his chair to wrap her arm around him.

'Oh?' He raised a surprised brow. 'She did?'

'She told me just last week. We had a little chat together and she also said, despite everything, she'd never stopped loving her Bertie.'

Pa nodded. 'Yes, that was true. She always showed me her love even when I was misbehaving.' He gave a wry chuckle.

'Then that's settled,' Michael nodded. 'You go

and get your stuff from the pub, and move back into your old bedroom.'

Angeline watched as the lines of worry on her father's face smoothed over. Just knowing that he was loved and accepted by his family was all he needed right now.

***

It was just a few days later when Angeline was getting ready to go to work at Mrs Featherstone's house when there was a sharp knock on the door. Pa had already left to go to seek employment again by enquiring around the shops and big houses in the area if they needed any help with a view to taking him on. He had a key, so it couldn't be him. Michael had left early too and Angeline was due to take Sammy and Joanna to school on her way. So the sudden intrusive knock startled her. It was something she could do without as she was running behind time.

She told her brother and sister to take a seat at the table while she went to see who it was, she hoped it was someone she could get rid of quickly.

But as she drew the door open to see the young woman standing there who was probably only a few years older than Eliza, she felt her stomach lurch as by the look on the woman's face, it wasn't good news.

'Where's that no-good father of yours?' scowled the woman. Recognition dawned, it was the big-chested barmaid from the Kings Arms. She hadn't recognised her at first as the woman's usual long raven-haired locks were usually loose on her shoulders but now were covered by a shawl. What did she want Pa for?

'He's not here at the moment,' Angeline replied curtly, 'and I'm just about to set off for work.'

'You can give him a message for me!'

Angeline nodded, though in truth, was annoyed that the woman had dared to knock on their door after all that had gone on lately. Wasn't she aware that Ma had recently passed away? She had some front after her dalliance with Pa.

'You can inform that *Dear Daddy* of yours that he's left a bun in the oven!'

Angeline frowned. What did she mean by that? Had Pa been baking for the woman?

'A baby!' the woman yelled at her. 'Another bleedin' mouth to feed, so he'd better cough up fine style!'

Angeline's hands flew to her face in horror. She couldn't believe that there was a new baby sister or brother on the way. What on earth would Michael and Eliza make of that?

'You'll have to speak to him yourself!' Angeline shouted back at her. 'It's none of my flamin' business!' Then she shouted over her shoulder to her brother and sister. 'Come on kids, you'll be late for school!'

Both came scurrying past her and she locked the door behind them.

The woman stood there open-mouthed from the shock of the backchat from Angeline. That woman had wrecked things for them as a family, pulled them all apart, but then a little voice inside her said:

No, it was Pa who did that. He was the married one and he ruined it for you all.

She didn't know who to feel angriest with, the woman with the big mouth and big breasts or her father for getting them into all this bother? It was evident she was after money for herself and the baby, and goodness knew what else.

***

When Pa called to Mrs Featherstone's later that afternoon to walk Angeline home, she waited until they'd begun their journey before telling him about what had occurred earlier that morning. She didn't want Mrs Featherstone to catch wind of it until she'd spoken to her father.

The blood drained away from his face as she related what had gone on and his eyes grew large.

He opened his mouth and closed it again before clearing his throat to speak. 'I...I... don't know what to say. I haven't had any relations with Maisie since just after Christmas...' he said, shaking his head in disbelief.

As young as Angeline was, she knew all about the birds and the bees and that Pa had been having some sort of relationship with the young woman well before Ma's death, she'd seen the evidence of it for herself when she'd called into the Kings Arms to buy some brandy for her mother. The way her father had reacted when he'd seen her was all the evidence she'd needed of how close they'd become.

'I suppose I'm going to have to speak to her about it. I'm sorry, Angeline, you shouldn't have been dragged into it. It's my affair, not yours.' He shrugged his shoulders, and for the majority of the journey home, they walked in silence. Now Pa's mind was elsewhere, probably worrying about it all. Just when things were settling down having him back home with them.

***

As to be expected, Michael was upset on hearing the news but Eliza was more understanding and said maybe Maisie should be invited over for her to speak to Pa rather than on the doorstep or in the pub, Angeline tended to agree.

'Well, I'm having nothing to do with it,' Michael said angrily as he glared at his father. 'Ma's not cold in her coffin and you're already inviting that trollop here! And what about the baby? It'll be a bastard born out of wedlock!'

The look of hurt in Pa's eyes was evident.

'You take back what you said there!' yelled Eliza, while Angeline stood looking on. The house had been peaceful that morning before that woman had arrived, now what on earth was happening?

Michael grabbed his jacket from the hook on the back of the door.

'Where are you going?' Pa looked at his son and went to follow after him.

Michael turned to face his father. 'Anywhere out of this mad house!' he shouted, and then he was gone, banging the door, the sound of his boots clattering on the cobbles outside.

Angeline and Eliza exchanged worried glances with one another.

Trying to soften the blow, Angeline said, 'Come on, Pa. Sit yourself down. I'll put the tea on. It's corned beef stew.' But she could tell her father had no appetite for it. He wouldn't be right until he'd sorted things out with Maisie.

***

Pa rose from the armchair and headed for the door.

'Where are you off to?' Eliza looked at him as Angeline emerged from the scullery.

He turned to face them. 'I have to see the vicar.'

'But the stew is almost ready!' Angeline frowned at her father. She'd made it with a view to him eating it as he looked so thin and gaunt lately.

He paused for a moment and looking at both of his daughters said, 'I have to do the decent thing. I'm going to have a word about the situation with Reverend Aylward...'

Decent thing? What did Pa mean by that? Then it dawned on her as her eyes enlarged. He meant he'd have to marry the woman!

'But Pa,' Eliza put her hand on his shoulder, 'if you mean what I think you mean, that won't seem decent marrying her either, so soon after Ma's passed away.'

He shrugged his shoulders. 'What am I supposed to do? I'm damned if I do and damned if

I don't. At least this young child won't be let down by me like you all were.'

He grabbed his jacket and scarf from the back of the door, and removing his flat cap from his jacket pocket, slipped it on his head.

'Don't fret none, girls. I won't be gone too long, I'm just looking for advice, that's all.'

Angeline wrinkled her nose and then she looked at her sister as their father closed the door behind him. 'What do you reckon?'

'I hope he's not too hasty and ends up booking a bleedin' wedding for them both!'

'Surely not? Let's hope it's just advice he's gone for then.'

Eliza nodded. 'Come on, I'll lay the table for you and slice the loaf of bread. At least we can eat the stew, then I have to get back for George.'

Angeline smiled. Eliza had been playing the dutiful wife of late and seemed more industrious than she had when she'd been living with her own family, though she guessed maybe she had to be residing under someone else's roof. Maybe George's mother was putting her sister through her paces, or maybe Eliza viewed her as a good role model and was trying to make a good impression on her. Whatever was the case, being married to George suited her sister.

Sometimes, in the evenings, and especially in bed at night, she missed her. They often had little chats before falling asleep, relating stories to one another, laughing and giggling. Other times they sang softly in the darkness, songs they'd been taught by their own dear mother.

Now that Eliza was no longer assembling matchboxes, she was seeking a new job, even though George insisted she no longer needed to work and could help his mother at home. But Eliza was the sort who needed a little freedom, she didn't like being cooped in all day. To be fair to her, she was doing her best to seek a new job but was having the same sort of luck as Pa—she'd either arrive too late and discover the position already filled or there was that old chestnut of "Thanks for enquiring. We'll make a note on file of your address and if a suitable position comes up, we'll contact you." Angeline thought that was a fob off if ever there was one!

There was no sign of Pa returning, so after they'd all eaten and Eliza had gone home to George, Angeline safely tucked up Sammy and Joanna in bed, then she sat and waited for Michael to return home. He'd been annoyed earlier by the situation, probably because all of this was far too soon after the funeral and too painful for them to bear on top of everything else.

Pa returned just as Angeline was off to bed herself, his face looking drawn and his shoulders hunched. She put her arms around him and kissed him softly on the cheek. That was good, there was no whiff of alcohol on him, and he seemed steady and sober. She'd been discussing the situation with Eliza earlier and both were concerned he'd hit the bottle again.

'What did Reverend Aylward have to say, Pa?'

He removed his cap and slipped it into his pocket and then hung his jacket and scarf behind the door.

'He was very understanding actually. He already knew of my wrongdoing...'

Angeline blinked in disbelief. 'He knew?'

Pa nodded. 'Yes, I told him when that blinding light happened in the alleyway on that particular day. I felt the need to confess my sins then.'

'So, what did he think about what Maisie said?'

'He suggested I invite her to have a chat with him in his office at the church, both of us together I mean.'

'That sounds a good idea.'

'Yes, and it won't upset our Michael as much as bringing her here.'

Angeline touched her father's hand. She hated to see him like this. No matter what he'd done in the past, he was paying heavily for it right now.

'Come and sit down by the fireside and I'll dish that stew up for you now.'

'Just a little then,' he said, making his way to his favourite chair.

It was a start at least. She glanced at the mantel clock. It was almost nine o'clock, and Michael never stayed out this late without telling them in advance. Now her father was back home she ought to be a little happier but she was concerned about her brother's welfare, the way he'd stormed out of the house earlier. Was there a storm brewing? She sincerely hoped not.

Chapter Twenty Three

It was in the early hours of the morning that Angeline awoke, startled. For a moment, she was about to wake Eliza to ask her to go downstairs with her to investigate the strange noises sounding like pots being banged and the clattering of cutlery, as though someone was crashing around in the scullery. Then she remembered, her sister no longer shared a bedroom with her and it was probably Michael as by the time she'd drifted off to sleep, he'd still not returned home.

She swiftly donned her slippers and softly padded down the stairs, to see Michael sitting at the table shovelling down last night's stew from a saucepan. He glanced up at her as she approached and she felt a sickening lurch in the gut. This was too reminiscent of how Pa had been. Even before she drew close to him, she could smell the alcohol. So that's where he'd been—to the pub.

'Michael, are you all right?'

'Yes, good as gold. I didn't bother heating this soup up, I'm bleedin' starving,' he said with a grin. 'Tastes good cold though.' Lifting his spoon, he carried on with it.

'But where have you been all this time?' She

THE ANGEL OF CHRISTMAS ALLEY

blinked.

He stopped shovelling spoonfuls of stew into his mouth to look at her properly now. 'To the Kings Arms.' He was slurring his words and he needed to get up for work in the morning. She glanced at the clock on the mantelpiece, it was half past one and her brother needed to get up at half past six.

She bit on her lip as though deliberating what to say next, she didn't want to anger him as that's why he'd left the house in the first place. 'What made you go there?'

'Just fancied a drink I suppose.' He belched loudly as he rubbed his stomach and didn't even excuse himself. She was mortified at her brother's rude behaviour, he wasn't usually so uncouth.

'Was there another reason for going there?' She folded her arms as she awaited his response.

He raised a brow as he dipped a piece of bread into the saucepan, then made direct eye contact with her. 'How'd you mean?'

'Other than going there for a drink, were you going there to see someone?'

She had the feeling maybe he'd gone there to have a word with Maisie as she was behind the bar most evenings.

He nodded. 'To see the landlord.'

She frowned, not getting this at all. 'But why?'

He grinned at her. 'For someone so young you ask a lot of questions, our Angeline!'

'I'm entitled to as you weren't here for supper

and you've just woke me up with all your banging around.'

'Sorry. Look, I went there to see if I could rent Dad's old room and I stayed for a couple of drinks, that's all.'

It was more than a couple of drinks she reckoned. 'And?'

'And he said, yes I can rent the room.'

Her heart sank. 'But why are you leaving us now that we're all back together again?'

'I don't think I can live under the same roof as him, especially if he's now having a child with that woman. He'll be moving her in here next!' He raised his voice as his eyes surveyed the room.

That was something she hadn't considered that Maisie might be moved in with them but of course, that was a possibility as if he ended up making an honest woman out of her to save their child from illegitimacy, then that might well happen.

'He went to see the vicar after you left,' she said as she approached further, holding on to the back of one of the dining chairs as if for support.

Michael quirked a surprised eyebrow. 'He's wasting no time, is he? I reckon he had this all planned—get rid of the old girl and move the new one in. It's all been a bloody act. A comedy of errors!' He roughly pushed the saucepan away and rose to his feet.

'I don't think it's been an act, Michael. He seems genuine to me, that's a terrible thing to say!'

Michael seemed to have sobered up now as

his eyes flashed. 'Then if that's the case, how come she's pregnant all of a sudden? If he hasn't bothered with her for a while?'

'That can happen. Maybe it was before he left her.'

'Ha! I ruddy well doubt it. He's got his feet back under the table here now, well I won't be sticking around to live with no flippin' stepfamily. Now I'm off to my bed.'

'You won't leave without saying goodbye though, will you?' she asked, meekly.

Michael shot her a soft smile. 'No, of course I won't. And I'll pop around to see you when *he's* not at home.'

Angeline nodded. How could so much have changed in such a short space of time? She thought they finally had their father back as head of the family and all was going to be all right from now on. But things were far from all right, now there was a deep division which would only become greater if he married that woman and brought her to live with them.

Chapter Twenty Four

The following afternoon when Angeline had returned from a day of baking and delivering for Mrs Featherstone, she and Eliza were having a little chat at the table when there was a knock at the door. Her heart leapt, wondering if it was Michael returning having changed his mind about going to the digs at the pub. But when Eliza opened the door, it was Maisie who stood there.

Angeline drew up behind her sister to see what the woman had to say this time.

She seemed different now, not as aggressive and Angeline noticed her bottom lip was trembling as she spoke.

'Will you please tell your father I can't go with him to see the vicar today, some other time will have to do.'

Angeline elbowed her way past her sister so that she could face the woman. 'Why's that then?' She narrowed her gaze, realising her father was going out of his way to work things out between them for the sake of their unborn child.

Maisie swallowed hard. 'Just can't make it, that's all. I have to work at the pub.'

Angeline didn't believe a word of it. 'I reckon

you're saying that as you're not really having a baby!' she yelled at her, causing Eliza to grab hold of her sister's arm.

'Come on now, Angeline,' she said softly, 'this isn't helping.'

Maisie looked at Eliza and smiled nervously. 'No, it's not. I am telling the truth, I am pregnant.' She stood sideways and ran her hand over an obvious bump which caused Angeline to now regret her words.

'I'm sorry, I shouldn't have suggested that,' Angeline said, now trying to make amends. 'When could you make it then?'

'Not for another week or two. I'm rushed off me feet at the pub as we're so short-staffed.'

'That's all right,' said Eliza kindly. 'We'll tell Pa when he gets home.'

Maisie nodded at them and then turned her back to leave.

When the girls stepped inside the house and shut the door, Eliza turned to her sister. 'Why were you so horrible to her?'

Angeline shook her head. 'I don't know. I just feel she's lying about something. I accept there is a baby seeing her bump like that, but it's all very odd.'

'I know what you mean. Something doesn't add up, does it?'

'No. But what can we do about it?' Angeline gestured with her open palms.

'Nothing I suppose. I just hope Pa won't be

too disappointed when he finds out she won't be going to see the vicar with him. You'd think she'd bleedin' well jump at the chance as he could end up marrying her if the vicar's involved.'

'I know.'

***

Later that afternoon when Pa returned home after another day of unsuccessful job hunting, he seemed as flummoxed as his daughters were that Maisie had been unable to attend a meeting with the reverend at the church. And that she reckoned she was unavailable for the next couple of weeks, but he didn't speculate about the situation and spoke no more of it.

***

Angeline hadn't seen Tommy for such a long time as he was up early in the mornings to go to Covent Garden with Billy to select the best fruit and vegetables for their round, but today, Billy was having trouble with the cart again, so they both popped home for some refreshment while Billy attended to it.

'Are you enjoying working with Billy?' she asked him as she carefully placed some of Mrs Featherstone's currant buns into her wicker basket, covering them with a clean tray cloth.

Grinning at her, he spoke animatedly. 'Oh yes. I wish we hadn't had to stop right now as I'm loving it.'

She guessed he was good with the sales patter as he had been when he'd helped her to sell her matches.

'That's good to hear.' She beamed at him.

He ceased smiling for a moment. 'What about you though, Angeline? Is everything going all right for you? I don't mean working for Ma as I can see that's going well for you.' She nodded. 'I mean at home since your mother has died.'

She sighed loudly, much louder than she'd intended, somehow she couldn't help herself.

'No, not really. Pa's moved back in at home and everything was going well until a woman turned up at the door,' she said, lowering her voice as she felt ashamed to speak of it in front of his mother who was in the other room.

He frowned. 'What sort of woman?'

'The woman Pa was having a dalliance with when he was married to my mother.'

'Oh! I see.'

'Yes, she reckons she's having his baby and I think he might marry her to make an honest woman out of her.'

'You don't approve?' he studied her face.

'It's not whether I approve or not to tell you the truth, it's just that there's something about her I don't trust. I feel she's lying about something.'

'About the baby?'

'Not sure. I can see she's pregnant so that is true. I don't know maybe I'm just being daft, Tommy.'

'No, gal. Now you listen to me,' he draped a reassuring arm around her shoulders. 'If you feel there's something amiss, there probably is.

Keep your eyes and ears open until you think differently.'

She nodded. 'Thank you. I thought maybe it was my imagination.'

'No, I don't think so, love. It's your instinct telling you something's not right. My instincts have never failed me so far.'

She supposed that Tommy made a good point.

***

That evening, Pa returned home with a gleam in his eyes, it was the happiest Angeline had seen him in a long while.

'You'll never guess my good news!' He said, lifting her in his arms and swinging her around so she was giddy and breathless.

He set her down and grinned.

'No, Pa. What is it?'

'I've got a job, I've finally got a job at last!'

Angeline blinked several times. 'That's great news, Pa! How'd that come about?'

'Well, it was that lady from the big house, Mrs Billington, the one I went to see that first day when I thought she'd picked the younger applicant. Turns out she hadn't rebuffed me after all. I was her first choice. It's been a good couple of weeks, so I just assumed someone else was chosen.'

'That's brilliant news, Pa. Eliza will be ever so pleased for you.'

He nodded. 'Just not Michael though, eh?'

'He'll come around, you'll see.'

She hated the thought that Pa couldn't be truly

happy right now because he was concerned about Michael and the circumstances of having a child on the way. Nevertheless, Angeline thought it worth celebrating anyhow.

'I'm going to bake you a special cake, Pa,' she said. 'I'm that proud of you.' She had acquired some baking skills from Mrs Featherstone and knew how to bake some of the easier cakes the woman made as she'd shown her and even allowed her to bake a lemon sponge cake with desiccated coconut on the top last week and it had turned out fine, so that's what she was going to make for her father. There was a little shop down the road that would sell all the necessary ingredients.

She donned her shawl and bonnet and lifting her wicker basket from the table, said, 'I won't be long, Pa, I'll be back before you know it.'

He waved at her and smiled as he settled down in the armchair, no doubt about to take a nap in front of the fire. Pa had walked miles this past couple of weeks in his quest to get himself a job.

There was no desiccated coconut available at the shop, but they had all the other necessary ingredients, so Angeline purchased a bag of icing powder instead. She'd seen Mrs Featherstone add a spot of hot water to it for her iced buns. She could easily do the same. She was just about to round the corner to enter Christmas Alley, when she spotted someone familiar on the pavement opposite, chatting to a gentleman in a bowler hat who was now taking her by the arm and escorting her towards The Kings Arms. It was Maisie! And by the look on her face, she seemed to be quite unhappy to be in his presence. Who was he? She wondered.

It was getting dark and she should be home, but instead, she trailed the pair and watched them as he roughly pushed Maisie inside the pub. What was going on here?

There was no use in her hanging around any longer, Pa and the little ones would be wondering where she was, so she retraced her steps and headed off home.

***

The following evening, Angeline called to see Michael at the pub. She hadn't mentioned to Pa what she'd seen the previous evening not to upset his good news, but she had a plan that she just couldn't wait to hatch.

When she explained who she was to the landlord, he was more than happy to direct her through the bar and up the stairs to her brother's room. She'd never visited Pa there when he'd had the room, though, of course, Eliza had. There'd been no sign of Maisie at all behind the bar, so she was definitely fibbing about not being able to see the vicar with Pa. Yes, it was most certainly the landlord she'd seen with Maisie in the street yesterday and now she questioned the relationship.

A young woman with painted lips and with a garish dress sense, passed her on the landing. She looked a right sort. Common as muck, her Ma would have said.

When the woman had disappeared into her room, with a bottle of something, she'd no doubt purchased downstairs. Angeline knocked on Michael's door three times, before Michael emerged, opening it wide for her.

'Angeline!' he blinked several times, resting his hand on the door jamb. 'What on earth are you doing in a place like this?'

'I used to come here to get brandy for Ma, remember?'

'That's true enough, but you've never been upstairs in here before. There are all sorts staying at this place.'

It was obvious Michael feared for her safety being here.

'Well, you'd better invite me inside, then,' she said.

He nodded. 'What brings you here, though?'

She laid her basket on the table. 'I've brought you some of the cake I baked for Pa,' she said, drawing back the covering cloth to reveal a segment of the iced lemon cake.

Michael's eyes widened. 'That looks *so* good. And it's very thoughtful of you but what's the occasion? His birthday's not till August!'

'He's got himself a new job working for a lady in a big house.'

Michael raised his eyebrows as though he couldn't believe Pa had actually got himself a job.

'Well, let's hope he manages to keep it.'

'Also,' she said, 'I don't think that Maisie one working here is telling the truth about her baby being Pa's. I think it's either the landlord's or someone else's who comes here for a drink.'

Michael frowned. 'What makes you say that?'

'I noticed her walking with the landlord in the street last evening when I went to buy the cake ingredients from Mason's the grocery shop. He was being very familiar with her and it appeared as if she didn't like the attention. In the end, he practically pushed her into the pub. What's going on, Michael? And why did you warn me off coming here?'

'All right,' he said sighing deeply. 'It's not a nice place. There are ladies of the night working here, but I don't know if Maisie is one of them or not as I only go to the bar if she's not behind it.'

'Then you have to make an effort and keep your eyes and ears open for Pa's sake. If he marries her and she's lying, it will affect us all, including him.'

Her brother nodded as if he could see the sense of that. 'All right. I'll give the old fella the benefit of the doubt. Have a seat,' he said gesturing with his hand, 'and we'll have a slice of that cake, it looks delicious.'

And so, it was decided that Michael would have a drink now and again in the bar, just the one at most as Angeline had said she didn't want to see him in the same state as he was just recently, and he agreed with her. It had been difficult for him to work the following day with so much drink inside him and so little sleep before his shift.

He'd eavesdrop in the bar now and again without drawing attention to himself. Maisie had no idea who he was. It was a plan of sorts.

Chapter Twenty Five

Pa had settled down to work at the big house. Although Mrs Billington employed a butler, cook and a maid, someone was needed to step in to see to the house's repairs and maintenance as well as run errands for the woman—Albert Barker, seemed to fit the bill nicely.

He'd tried to make contact with Maisie, but for some reason the young woman was having none of it, telling the landlord not to allow him to set foot over the door of the premises.

In the end, he'd taken to writing her a letter, outlining his responsibilities as father of the child, but that seemed to have been ignored.

It all appeared a mystery to Angeline. Why come to their home in the first place, demanding her father take responsibility for the child and then go back on that?

Angeline visited Eliza at her parents' in-law home one afternoon after work. They were seated in the front room parlour that was now deemed as Eliza's and George's room. It was a decent size with a fire grate with alcoves on either side with shelves for various books and ornaments. New flowered chintz drapes had been fitted to the windows along with lace curtains for their privacy. Against the wall was a double bed and in front of the window, a small table with two chairs. There was also a small sofa and a walnut wardrobe with drawers beneath it to store their clothing. All in all, with the fire lit in the grate, Angeline thought it looked very cosy indeed. It was the first time she'd ever visited the property.

The sisters were seated at the table, with Eliza showing off her embroidery work. Mrs Whittle had painstakingly shown her all the various stitches, and to Angeline's surprise, her sister had really taken to it.

It was then, that Angeline felt the need to explain how odd things were about Maisie going back on wanting to see their father and how she'd seen her in the street that time with the landlord of the Kings Arms.

Eliza frowned. 'It sure is strange. I mean Pa went to all that trouble to try to get her to see the vicar with him. There was a strong possibility he'd have wed her an' all to save her from shame.'

Angeline nodded. 'Don't worry, Michael's on the case as he's staying at the pub, he said he'll keep his eyes and ears open. He thinks it most odd as well.'

'How is Pa doing since working for Mrs Billington? I'll have to pop over to visit him soon.'

Angeline blinked. 'At the big house?'

'No!' Eliza laughed as she tossed her red glossy locks. 'At home, silly. I'd never dare to knock on the front door of a house like that.'

Angeline smiled. It was good to see her sister laughing once again. They hadn't had much to laugh about since Ma passed away.

'It'll be good for him to see you. The kids too.'

'How are they doing?' Eliza set down her embroidery as though very interested in their welfare.

'Oh good. Sammy is finally reading well and Joanna's pleased as she came top of her class in spelling.'

'She's so much like you, Angeline. A little bookworm. Not like me, this is the only talent I have,' she said, lifting her embroidery and turning it to face Angeline. 'That and making ruddy matchboxes!' She shot her sister a wry smile.

Angeline reached out for Eliza's hand across the table. 'Don't put yourself down. I think your embroidery is beautiful. Maybe you ought to ask Mrs Featherstone if you can help her with the garments she makes or go to work in a sewing factory?'

Eliza nodded. 'Yes, maybe that would be a good idea!' Her eyes lit up at the mention of it.

Angeline hoped she had planted a little acorn in her sister's mind that would grow into a great oak tree someday.

'How's George getting on?'

'He's enjoying working at the docks but...' she bit her lower lip.

'But what?'

'I don't know that he'd like me to go to work.

His idea is for me to stay at home all day and help his mother look after the house. He reckons there's enough wages coming in to allow me to do that what with his own, his father's and the money his brothers bring in.'

'It's nice to be in that position if that's what you truly want?'

'That's just it though, I've never been very domesticated, have I?'

Angeline chuckled. 'No! I can definitely vouch for that!'

Her sister began to chuckle too. At least things were going well for her and Angeline was happy about that.

***

It was a few days later when Michael brought the news that he thought there was most certainly something going on with Maisie and the landlord. He'd been in the bar one night and when they must have thought they weren't being watched, he noticed the man, who looked old enough to be her father, slip his hand around her waist and kiss the back of her neck. They'd been near the entrance to the hallway behind the bar at the time and probably thought no one could see, but he had. But then again, he'd been looking out for such behaviour. No one else appeared to have noticed. Michael had got to know a lot of the pub regulars and he knew at least one of them would have said something if they'd witnessed what he had.

The following evening after work, he called to

LYNETTE REES

the house just ten minutes after his father had arrived home.

As Michael thrust open the door, Pa looked up at him from the armchair as Angeline came rushing out from the scullery with a saucepan of potatoes in her hand. She'd been about to dish them up for Pa along with a lamb chop and peas for his supper. But the way the door had burst open like that, and the look of anxiety on her father's face, had caused her great alarm.

'It's all right,' said Michael calmly, showing his vertical palms as though in defence as he approached his father who was now sitting bolt upright in his chair. 'I come in peace.'

'Funny sort of peace!' said Angeline as her chin jutted out. 'We don't need you to frighten us like that this time of a night! You haven't been drinking again, have you?'

He chuckled and shook his head.

'Sit down then, lad,' said their father.

Michael nodded and then he removed his jacket and cap. Angeline having laid the saucepan on the table, took them from him and hung them up on the back of the door.

Michael took the stool opposite his father. 'The first thing I'd like to say Pa, is sorry. I've misjudged you and your intentions...'

Pa's mouth gaped wide open now at the surprise of it all. He closed it, then said, 'Why the sudden turnaround and bursting in here like a raving banshee?'

'Sorry. I didn't mean to startle either of you, but there's something you should know. You too, Angeline.'

She drew closer and took a seat on the arm of her father's chair.

Now both sets of eyes were on Michael.

'I don't think that baby Maisie is carrying is yours, Pa.'

Pa raised his eyebrows and swallowed. 'Whyever not? Did she tell you so?'

Michael shook his head. 'No. But Angeline saw her with the landlord of the Kings Arms in the street recently and got suspicious at the way they were acting together.'

Pa glanced across at her. 'You never told me.'

Angeline shrugged her shoulders. 'It was the evening you got the good news about your job and I went to buy some things to bake that cake for you. It was only a suspicion and I didn't want to ruin the occasion.'

He nodded. Then gazing intently at Michael said, 'Go on, son...'

'Well, she told me about it and asked me to keep a watch over what was going on. I saw some evidence last night with my own eyes that they're more than friendly with one another. I don't think they realised anyone had clocked them. Pa, you have got to confront her about this or else you might be taken for a mug.'

Pa's face reddened. 'I might go to the pub and have a word with the landlord if she won't speak to me!'

'You'd better take me with you then,' said Michael firmly, 'seeing as how lately she's been avoiding you and saying you mustn't be allowed in the pub.'

'Very well, son. Can I meet you outside there, say about seven o'clock tomorrow evening?'

'Aye. That suits me.'

It was good to see both father and son making up with one another, though Angeline now wondered if her brother would ever return home again.

*****

'You look like you've got the weight of the world on yer shoulders!' Tommy looked at Angeline with concern in his brown eyes. They were both stood outside his home at the top of the cellar steps. Angeline had paused to speak to him on her way to deliver that morning's cakes to The Silver Kettle tea shop.

She shrugged, knowing full well how right he was. Tommy had returned to his house to get a change of clothing as he'd got soaked to the skin on the way to and from Covent Garden that particular morning. But now it had stopped raining and the sun was making an appearance, so he'd changed into a dry pair of corduroy trousers, a woollen shirt, a leather waistcoat and a spotted neckerchief just like his brother wore. In some respects, Angeline thought he was like a smaller version of Billy and the lad liked to mimic his behaviour too. He looked up to all his older brothers and fair play, they all treated him well.

'Sorry if I sound a bit glum. It's just I'm worried about my father.'

'You mean since your mother's death?'

'Not just that, but he has some other trouble brewing.' She didn't want to say too much in case they were overheard, but she knew she could trust Tommy.

'Tell me about it then, love.'

Letting out a long sigh, she said, 'It's that woman Pa had a relationship with who claims to be carrying his baby. We think she's lying though but we don't know why.'

Tommy raised his eyebrows. 'Funny sort of thing to lie about, if you ask me.'

Angeline nodded. 'I suppose so. Like I said previously, Pa would offer to marry her, to do the decent thing but all of a sudden she's avoiding him.'

'That is strange behaviour indeed!'

'Not only that but Michael and me have both seen her having a dalliance with the landlord of the pub she works for.'

'Ooooh! She's a spicy one!'

'You can say that again. Anyhow, my concern for Pa is if it all gets too much for him whether he'll hit the bottle again.'

'I see. Not a good time for this to happen after your Ma has just passed away.'

'No, it's not. Anyhow, I have to put it out of my

mind for time being. I need to ask your mother something.'

'Oh?' Tommy's eyes rounded like two saucers.

'It's our Eliza. She needs a job and she's developed a talent for embroidery and such. I was wondering if your mother would take her on to help with her sewing side of the business?'

Tommy shrugged his shoulders. 'Dunno if she would, you can only ask I suppose.' With his hands dug deep in his pockets, he absently kicked the wrought iron railings surrounding the cellar steps with the tip of his boot.

Angeline supposed he was right. But when would be the best time? She thought about it briefly, deciding to ask the woman when she returned from the delivery. Best to strike while the iron was hot.

Looking at Tommy, she said, 'Don't worry about me, I'll be all right.'

'I know you will, love. You're a little smasher!' he grinned at her, causing her cheeks to flame, but as she turned to walk away, she had a little smile on her face.

***

To Angeline's surprise, Mrs Featherstone had been agreeable to Eliza helping her out. She said she'd teach her all she knew and if she was up to scratch, she might even buy or rent another machine so she might expand her business. Angeline couldn't wait to tell her sister, but first, there was something she needed to do and do it quickly.

She realised that evening Pa would be meeting Michael outside The Kings Arms so he'd be allowed inside and get to speak with Maisie. Angeline hadn't been too sure that would be a good idea, and in any case, she wasn't happy about Pa going inside a pub, there was just too much temptation for him.

So, instead, she decided she was going to confront Maisie herself, deciding to call there on her way home from work, before picking up the kids from school. As she reached The Kings Arms, she noticed the swing doors open and close as though someone had just stepped inside. The foul mingle of alcohol and smoke almost caused her to gag. She realised she was too young to go to such a place but it was all in a good cause. She'd already called there recently, even if it was just upstairs looking for Michael, she could do the same thing again, even if it did remind her of Ma, getting her daily tot of brandy for her.

Taking her courage in both hands, she pushed open the door and stepped inside, her eyes scanning the room. In one corner there was a group of men who were playing some sort of card game. So intent in their pursuit that they barely looked up to notice her presence. In another corner was a woman in a gaudy red dress with her bosom almost spilling over the top of it. She was in the company of a much older man who seemed to have his hands all over her. Angeline forced her eyes shut for a moment, to try to block out the image, then she opened them again.

Turning her head, she made her way to the bar. Of course, she was familiar with the place as it was here she came to for those tots of Ma's brandy when she'd first taken sick but now Ma was no longer here, it was painful for her. Taking a deep breath, she composed herself.

The landlord was behind the bar, drying a pint glass with a cloth and he looked up at her approach.

'Hello young lady, what can I do for you?'

'Please Mister, I don't want no alcohol or anything, I would just like a word with Miss Maisie.' She had no idea of the woman's surname.

He shot her an amused smile, setting down the glass and cleaning cloth on the bar. 'I'll just fetch her for you,' he said. Then he turned and walked off towards the hallway arch, just behind the bar.

As Angeline gazed around the place, she wondered why on earth her father had wanted to spend so much of his time here for? It was a foul-smelling place, but then his reason appeared by her side when she turned her head.

Maisie! But this didn't look like the feisty young woman who stood outside her door a few days ago, screeching in her face. Now she seemed subdued. And what was that bruise on her cheekbone?

'You wanted to speak to me?' She glanced behind herself in the landlord's direction as though petrified of the man. Angeline hoped now she wasn't getting her into trouble. And was he responsible for that bruise?

Angeline nodded. 'I have to ask you something in private,' she said quietly, so as not to be overheard.

'All right, it's difficult for me to speak in here right now, but I'll meet you in ten minutes by the alleyway to your house.'

Angeline smiled and nodded, feeling some compassion for the woman for the first time. It couldn't be easy being stood behind that bar for all hours in her condition.

She turned her back and heard the landlord shout, 'What did the young girl want?'

'Oh, she just had a message for me from my sister, that's all, Fred. I have to pop out for a few minutes soon to fetch her a bottle of cough medicine. Is that all right?'

'Yes, but keep it short as we'll get busy soon.'

Poor Maisie having to lie like that. It was obvious she feared Fred. Angeline made her way across the road to the alleyway and waited. It was some time before Maisie showed up, breathless. She looked freezing cold, as she clutched her shawl around her shoulders, her teeth chattering.

'Come inside the house,' Angeline urged. 'The fire won't be lit as I've been working all day but it'll be warmer than out here.'

Maisie nodded gratefully. 'Thank you, darlin'.'

Angeline led her down the alley and unlocked the door to allow her in. 'Sit by there in the armchair,' she said with a smile. 'Would you like something hot to drink?'

Maisie slowly lowered her pregnant form into the armchair with a little huffing and puffing. 'No, not for me thanks as I ain't got the time or Mr Blackthorne will be on the warpath.'

'Fred?'

'Yes, the landlord.'

Angeline nodded and sat in the opposite armchair, leaning forward to speak to her with her hands clasped before her. She was going to have to light the fire soon so they'd have some warmth for the evening.

'What is it you've brought me here for, eh?'

'My name's Angeline.' She drew in a long breath and slowly released it. This was going to be awkward. 'You know how Pa asked you to go with him to see the vicar to discuss your er, um, situation together?'

Maisie nodded. 'Yes.'

'Why haven't you gone with him?'

Maisie's face paled at Angeline's direct form of questioning.

'I didn't have the time.'

'But it sounds to me as though he might marry you for the sake of the baby.'

A light flush spread over Maisie's cheeks. 'I'm sorry I can't answer your question.'

For a moment, Angeline thought the woman might cry. 'Why not?'

'You're only a young slip of a girl, that's why. This is something that doesn't concern you.'

THE ANGEL OF CHRISTMAS ALLEY

'I might only be a slip of a girl as you say, but I've had to be a mother to my family since my Ma got sick and passed away, and especially since Eliza and Michael have now left home…' she said with a catch in her voice now.

'Very well,' said Maisie in a softer tone. 'I wasn't telling the truth about the baby being your father's.'

'But why would you lie like that and upset us all, particularly after my mother died?' Angeline tilted her head to one side as she waited for the woman's answer.

'Because if it was anyone's baby I'd have wanted it to be your father's, he showed me a lot of kindness. It's Fred's baby and well, he knocks me around a little as you can see.' She pointed to her cheek.

Angeline gasped as she studied the bruise more closely, it was yellow and blue. 'But he shouldn't do that to a woman at all never mind a pregnant one.'

'I know but I started out working as one of his girls upstairs, if you know what I mean?'

Angeline knew very well what she meant after what Michael had told her about that place. 'So why don't you just leave?'

'Where would I go to, luvvy? I have no one to help me.'

'Your sister's?'

'She has problems of her own. She was like your Ma working at that match factory and she's got a cough as well.'

So Pa had obviously told Maisie about Ma's illness. 'It's not easy when someone is very ill like that. Is that why you mentioned about the cough medicine to the landlord?'

'Yes. It's true though I do have to get it when I leave here. I'll check on her kids at the same time as her husband will be at work.'

Poor Maisie, the woman she'd seen as being carefree in the past as she'd flirted behind the bar with the men at the pub, wasn't as carefree after all.

'Don't think too badly of me, Angeline, will you?'

'I won't,' said Angeline with a smile. 'I don't. But can I tell Pa what you've told me?'

'Yes, for sure. I came to my senses about lying about the baby when he asked me to go to the church to speak to the vicar. I could never bring meself to tell an untruth in the house of God.'

Angeline nodded, then she helped Maisie to her feet and escorted her to the door. As she watched her leave, she hoped all would go well for her, but somehow she doubted it.

Chapter Twenty Six

Pa and Michael were both pleased to hear the news that Maisie had admitted the baby she was carrying was the landlord's. Now there was no need for them to go to the pub to see the woman after all.

'That Fred Blackthorne is a right 'un from what I can make of him,' said Michael with a sneer, 'handy with his fists an' all whenever a fight breaks out on the premises.'

'He's handy with his fists all right!' yelled Angeline. 'Maisie's got a nasty bruise on her face from one of them.'

'Oh no!' said Pa. 'We have to get her some help. I'll ask the vicar does he know of anyone who might provide assistance.'

'Might be a good idea,' said Angeline. 'Now then as you're both here, why don't I go out and get us some hot pies for supper?'

Both nodded. 'That sounds good,' said Michael, 'but I'll go and fetch them. Don't want you out in the dark walking on your own, young lady.' He scolded good-naturedly.

Angeline smiled, hoping things could settle

down again and the drama leave them well and truly behind for once.

'You know, darlin',' Pa said directing his gaze at Angeline, as he sat between Sammy and Joanna on the couch, Sammy had been showing him a book he'd been given at school, and Joanna had been sitting listening intently, 'I'm so content being back home with you all. I can't believe how much I missed of you all growing up because of my behaviour.'

'Well, you're here now Pa.' Angeline smiled. 'And that's all that matters from now on. You like working for Mrs Billington too?'

'Oh yes.' His eyes left her for a moment as Sammy turned the page on his book to show Pa a picture.

'That's good.' She was so pleased the kids were happy sitting on either side of their father.

Pa looked up again. 'She's a fair employer. The rest of the staff are nice to me too.'

'That's all that matters then, Pa. I'm going to warm up some potatoes and carrots I have left over from last night's meal, they'll go nicely with the pies.'

He nodded at her and then turned his attention back to the two younger ones.

Angeline couldn't help dwelling on Maisie though, every time she tried to think about something else, her mind would return to the young woman and what she must be going through at the pub with that landlord.

She absently scooped a bowl of previously cooked potatoes and carrots into a pan and fried them in a little lard ready for Michael's return. By the time she'd have finished warming those and setting the table, he would most probably have returned.

But half an hour later when he still hadn't come back, and the children's stomachs were growling with hunger, Pa and Angeline exchanged concerned glances with one another.

'I can't understand where he'd have got to?' Pa frowned. 'I hope he hasn't gone off to a pub somewhere.'

'I doubt that, Pa,' said Angeline. 'Michael was just as hungry as the rest of us.'

Pa rose from the couch. 'I'm going to go out and look for him. I'll call to the pie shop first and if he's not there, then I'll try the Kings Arms in case there's some reason he had to return to his digs.'

'All right.' Angeline huffed out a breath. She didn't want her father to have to go out after working a long shift at the big house and particularly to a pub, but someone had to stay and look after the kids. And, besides, it wouldn't be safe for her to traipse around the streets in the dark as she passed through various courts and alleyways.

'I'll try not to be too long,' said Pa winking at her. 'No doubt they ran out of hot pies at the shop and he's gone off elsewhere to try to get some.'

Angeline nodded. 'Aye, maybe.' She didn't feel very convinced though it was as if she could sense something was up, but she didn't know what that something was. There was just a feeling of deep unease within herself. Her stomach fluttered at what might have happened to her brother.

***

It was a good hour later when Pa returned home. Meantime, Angeline had given the fried potatoes and carrots to her brother and sister. They had both whined throughout the meagre meal that they'd been promised a pie each that in the end she had lost her temper and shouted at them, then burst into tears of confusion. She ended up sweetening both of them up by making them cups of hot chocolate before bed which was usually a treat, but she did feel bad about raising her voice to them. Now both were safely tucked up in bed as Pa came in through the door, removing his cap and shutting the door behind himself.

He approached Angeline with a grave look on his face as he still held his flat cap in his hand.

'Pa?'

'Michael's been taken to the police station...' he said solemnly. He swallowed hard.

'But why? What's he done? He only went out to buy some pies for our supper.'

'It's Maisie.'

She noticed for the first time that her father's eyes were glistening with tears. 'Michael's been arrested as Maisie was found dead at the back of the pub, in the yard.'

'That's dreadful.' For a moment, she just

couldn't comprehend the situation as not that long ago, less than a few hours since, she'd been talking to the young woman who'd been sitting in their living room. 'B...b....but I don't understand, what was he doing at the pub anyhow?'

'Well, he must have gone back there to get some more money to purchase those pies is my guess. He's not the only one from the pub what's been arrested, mind. There are several. One of the other barmaids told me all about it when I called there to look for him. I suppose they have to question those men who were involved with the place, customers an' all.'

'And especially the landlord,' said Angeline as she pursed her lips.

'Yes, especially him.'

'Well we're not going to be getting any pies tonight,' said Angeline as she shot her father a wry smile. 'There's some leftover fried potatoes and carrots. I can open a tin of corned beef and make corned beef hash, if you like?'

Pa shook his head. 'I wouldn't have the stomach for it tonight after all that's gone on. Some tea and toast will do.'

Angeline nodded. The truth was, she didn't have the stomach for it either when she thought of what had happened to that poor young woman, it just didn't bear thinking about. It was like a bad dream, one she wasn't really taking in at present.

***

It wasn't until the following morning when she

rose for work that Michael returned to the house asking if he could come back to live with them all. He had no inclination to set foot in that pub ever again.

It transpired that he wasn't really in the frame for the murder but one or two customers along with the landlord at the pub, were still being held.

'Should I go to see the police about what Maisie told me yesterday about the bruise being from Fred Blackthorne?' Angeline asked Michael.

Michael slowly nodded his head. 'Aye. Best give them that information as it will clearly have a bearing on the case. I have to get ready for work in a minute.'

'No, you're not going,' said Pa firmly. 'I'll take Angeline to the police station first and then on my way to work, I'll call to see Mr Styles and explain the circumstances to him. From what I know of the man, he'll be very understanding.'

Michael smiled, gratefully. 'To be honest, I don't know if I have the strength to stand behind the counter to serve customers today, never mind take out any deliveries after the night of questioning I had last night. Thankfully, Mrs Rumble at the pie shop saw me around the time it happened.'

'Oh?' Pa raised his brow.

'Yes, I got as far as the pie shop and went to order from her, then realised I didn't have enough money to pay. I told her I'd slip back to the pub to get some money from my room. They'll probably question her later. By the time I arrived at the pub, all hell had broken loose as poor Maisie's body had been found in the yard and the constabulary had arrived.'

Angeline closed her eyes firmly shut at the image of the young woman's battered body in her mind. And what about the baby? That would have undoubtedly lost its life too as he or she would have been too young to survive without the safety of his or her mother's womb.

She couldn't help thinking how tragic it was and just how fragile life was for them all.

***

Eliza had now been taken on by Mrs Featherstone as her sewing assistant. For the first time, Angeline noticed how settled the girl had now become. She really had a flair for being a seamstress.

Mrs Featherstone though had been going missing several times over the past couple of weeks. Angeline had no idea what was going on. She was left in charge of some of the baking and she'd even encouraged Eliza to complete a gown for her, allowing her to add the lace trim to it. She must have great faith in us both, thought Angeline.

But although the woman seemed happy enough, it did concern her that something was amiss, maybe. Perhaps she was going to see a physician? She had appeared a little tired of late. Was that the reason they were being entrusted with tasks the woman would normally undertake herself? Was it all getting too much for her?

Then one Friday morning, Mrs Featherstone began to get ready to depart again. She'd picked up her best shawl that was draped across the dining chair, arranging it neatly around her shoulders. She also wore her Sunday best brown and cream bonnet with satin ribbons which she tied neatly beneath her chin.

Angeline exchanged glances with her sister as if to say, 'Here we go again. Where's she off to this time?'

She opened her mouth to say something but the woman was heading for the door. Turning, she smiled at both girls. 'I'll only be an hour or so. You make sure you have a break soon. There are some leftover buns from yesterday in the pantry and be sure to make yourselves a hot drink. You hear now, girls?'

Both nodded in her direction.

She turned her back and was gone through the door. Angeline watched her from the window where she could see her ascending the cellar steps. She glanced at Eliza.

'What do you think?'

Eliza laid down the gown she was attaching a lace collar to and frowned. 'Something's up for sure. Mrs Featherstone seems to have a lot on her mind of late.'

'I'm worried in case she's ill. She's looking quite tired lately.'

Eliza stood, and moving away from the treadle

machine, laid a hand on her sister's shoulder. 'Try not to fret too much. Can't you have a word with Tommy about it? Explain how worried we are about his mother and ask if there's anything we ought to be aware of?'

Angeline shrugged. 'I suppose so.'

'Now then, you heard what Mrs Featherstone said, we're to have a break. We need to abide by her wishes and keep things nicely ticking over for her here, no matter what's going on with her.'

Angeline nodded, supposing that her sister was quite right. So for time being, she pushed all thoughts of her employer's private affairs out of her mind. It wasn't until Tommy returned that afternoon to pick up a couple of sacks of potatoes for the cart that she questioned him about what was going on. Unfortunately, he had no idea either and as he wasn't home during the day, had no notion his mother had been leaving both girls to it for hours on end this past few days.

It was a full three and a half hours before Mrs Featherstone returned, her cheeks flushed and pinched from the cold outside, and she looked half frozen to death.

'Come and sit down,' said Angeline, leading the woman over to the armchair nearest the fire.

'All right, just let me get my breath,' said the woman as slowly, she removed her shawl and bonnet and hung them on the wooden coat stand beside the door.

'There's still some tea left in the pot,' said Eliza

with a hesitant smile on her face for she too, had now become concerned about the absences the woman was taking from the home.

'That would be lovely,' said Mrs Featherstone as she slowly eased herself into the armchair.

When she'd settled herself and Eliza had brought a cup of tea over, Angeline felt she had to ask as she knelt on the fireside rag rug in front of her.

'Is everything all right, Mrs Featherstone?'

'Why, of course it is, young lady! She chuckled. 'What did you think might be wrong, then?'

Angeline blinked. 'It's just that you're spending such a long time out of the house lately that I wondered, I mean, I thought perhaps you were going to see a physician as you're unwell.'

'Oh, dearie, dearie me!' Mrs Featherstone spluttered on her cup of tea. 'That's far from the case, lovely girl.' She patted Angeline on the head and placed her cup and saucer down on an occasional table beside her. Then looking into her eyes said, as the flames of the fire made them shine, 'It's not bad news at all. I'm sorry if I've made you think that. All will be revealed in good time, though.'

Angeline raised her eyebrows. What on earth did the woman mean by that? She felt it rude to pry, so she just smiled and nodded. Then she rose to her feet.

'I'm glad there's nothing wrong. I'm just off to deliver the final batch of cakes today.'

'Very well. You go home then, Angeline. Is your father collecting you today?'

'Er no, he has a lot on today. He's got to run some errands for Mrs Billington as she's planning some sort of party.'

Angeline watched the woman's face fall. Lately, Mrs Featherstone and Pa had been having lots of little chats when he called to pick her up and walk her home. The woman seemed a little disappointed he wasn't doing the same today.

'He'll be here tomorrow to pick me up then, though,' added Angeline which caused the woman to beam from ear to ear. It made her realise the woman did have a fancy for Pa and if she did, who was she to discourage such a thing? They were both widowed and possibly, although surrounded by family, lonely for a companion of sorts.

***

Over the following months, Mrs Featherstone's mysterious disappearances became less frequent, until they finally stopped altogether, though Angeline couldn't help feeling the woman had some sort of secret the rest of them weren't privy to.

She also noticed that now she and Pa seemed to be getting very familiar with one another. Once, she even found him at the house when she'd returned from her cake round. Without either hearing her approach, she had paused at the front door and heard voices inside. Eliza had not been on the premises as she'd already returned home to

LYNETTE REES

George. Pa was waiting to escort Angeline home again, but this time had turned up a little earlier. It was almost as though he'd sensed they'd be alone.

'Yes, Iris,' he was saying. 'I could get us a couple of tickets for the music hall on Saturday night, now what do you say?'

So, Mrs Featherstone's name was Iris! Angeline hadn't even realised that. She waited to hear the woman's reply before opening the front door.

'Oh, that would be smashing, Bertie. Simply smashing. I haven't had a night out in ever such a long time, not since my Joseph was alive.'

'Well, there you go. Saturday night it is, then!' Pa was replying enthusiastically.

Angeline smiled to herself, and then putting her hand on the doorknob, she opened the door.

When she entered, all was quiet as both pairs of eyes were directed towards her. A faint blush crept over Mrs Featherstone's cheeks and Pa was smiling. She'd done right to hold back before coming in, else the moment might have been lost to the pair.

'Hello, darlin'!' Pa greeted. 'I'll walk you home in a moment. I've just been discussing my plan to take Mrs Featherstone to the music hall on Saturday night as she deserves a good night out after all she's done for my girls!'

Mrs Featherstone fluttered her eyelashes coquettishly like a young girl, causing Angeline to smile even further. It was good to see both of them so happy.

'I'll just take this basket to the scullery then I'll be ready to go, Pa!'

Her father nodded and then turned his attention back to Mrs Featherstone once again. She could hear him telling the woman all about the act with top billing on Saturday night. He reckoned the man had come all the way from America.

Mrs Featherstone seemed enthralled with all the information Pa was giving her. He was a bit of a raconteur on the quiet.

***

The weather was getting warmer now as summer was on the horizon as trees were in full bud and the skies often a cerulean blue. The nights were longer too and the sounds of children playing in the streets now returned as it wasn't too cold to be outside.

'Pa,' Angeline said as she linked arms with him on their way home to Christmas Alley. 'Do you know what's been going on with Mrs Featherstone?'

Pa stopped in his tracks for a moment to take a look at his daughter. 'How'd you mean?'

'Well, for a few weeks, she kept disappearing, gone for hours on end leaving me and Eliza to it, but now that appears to have stopped…'

Pa let out a breath. 'I do have some idea, yes. But it's for her to tell you, not me. And she will in good time. I don't wish to break her confidence.'

'All right then, Pa. As long as it's nothing bad.'

He shook his head. 'No, it's nothing bad at all,' he

said.

They carried on walking in companionable silence past the tannery and a couple of factories belching out smoke. But today, everything looked cleaner, brighter somehow.

When they'd almost reached home, Pa paused again. 'I heard a whisper today...' he said with a grave look on his face, causing Angeline's heart to almost leap out of her chest.

'It's the landlord of The Kings Arms. There's to be a trial for Maisie's murder. He and a couple of his associates will be up in the dock. There's a good chance he'll swing for it.'

Angeline took a sharp intake of breath, knowing full well that Pa meant the man might be hanged. She nodded at her father, unsure of what to say as she released a steadying breath.

Finally, she said, 'How do you feel about all of that now? I mean as you and Maisie were once close.' She chose her words carefully.

'It all seems a lifetime ago, to be truthful. I just wish...' Pa's voice had a catch to it.

'Wish what, Pa?'

He swallowed hard. 'I just wish I'd realised how much danger she was in with that landlord. He must have been a jealous sort I reckon as she got a lot of attention from the men at the pub. If only...' He shook his head.

'I suppose we may never know.' There were many "if onlys" to ponder that would drive them all mad if they considered them all.

'Come on, Pa,' she said, linking her arm with his. 'How do you fancy some bubble and squeak for your tea? I've got some leftover veg and onion from yesterday's meal. I can fry that and warm up that bit of beef too.'

'Aye, I'd love that,' he said. 'You are too good to me, Angeline.' He planted a kiss on her forehead.

Chapter Twenty Seven

It was the end of November and Fred Blackthorne had gone to the gallows the previous month for his most heinous crime of murder. In some ways, Angeline felt it was now time for Pa to lay the past to rest. Maybe it was time for them all to do that. What a difference to this time last year when he'd been dragging them all out in the cold weather so he could get some extra pennies to buy a few pints.

Bobby was still happily living with Mr and Mrs Sampson and they were applying to legally adopt the lad so that they had the protection of the law on their side should anything untoward happen again in that respect. Though to be fair, the lad's uncle had not approached him since, despite knowing where he now lived.

Eliza was looking well of late, her cheeks had roses in them as Ma would have said, it was good to see her happy and content. She was becoming an expert seamstress who took great pride in her work.

Michael was being given more responsibility at the shop by Mr Styles and there was a small increase in his pay packet too.

Angeline felt that things were going so well

for them all that something dreadful just had to happen.

The shops and marketplace were now decorated with boughs of holly and mistletoe, and there was a general spirit of festivity in the air. Pa had taken to whistling Christmas Carols around the place. These days his interests were in the family and the Church as well as Mrs Featherstone!

Angeline was busier than ever supplying shops, tea rooms and offices with festive bakes such as mince pies, slices of iced Christmas cake and Yule chocolate logs. Eliza had helped Mrs Featherstone create a few fancy ballgowns for the young ladies from the big houses in the area and soon, there was a waiting list of ladies waiting to have a bespoke gown made especially for them for Christmas events.

So it was with some trepidation, when Mrs Featherstone summoned them all including her own family, Pa, Eliza, Angeline, Michael and the little ones, to her home on Christmas Eve, that something might have gone wrong? Was the woman about to say she was closing down her business as she couldn't cope with the demand?

Angeline shot Pa a nervous glance, while Michael, and Tommy and his elder brothers seemed mystified.

'I've asked you all here today to share some news with you...' the woman began as Pa walked over to her side and she looked up at him and smiled.

'Albert,' she said looking at her sons, 'your

father, girls, Michael...' she said now directing her
gaze at Pa's offspring, 'has proposed marriage to
me, and I've accepted.'

There was a long silence and for a moment,
Angeline thought that maybe it was such a shock
to everyone that they wouldn't like it. But the
opposite was true. Tommy and his brothers came
over to their mother's side and each planted a kiss
on her cheek, and then they shook Pa's hand.

Eliza appeared a little confused to begin with
but gradually she smiled and ran to Pa's side and
hugged him.

Pa looked at Angeline, Michael and the two little
ones. 'I hope you don't mind?'

'Mind? I've always been for it. I realised about
you two some months ago,' Angeline chuckled and
everyone else joined in.

Sammy and Joanna ran to Pa and he hugged
them to his side. They didn't appear to object
either as Michael stood there and nodded
approvingly.

'Now there's more,' said Mrs Featherstone.
'We're hoping to wed in the spring...'

'How lovely,' said Eliza, clasping the palms of
her hands together.

Angeline guessed they were waiting until then
as it would be over a year since Ma had passed
away, so that would seem a respectable amount of
time.

'That's not the main thing I was about to say,'
Mrs Featherstone continued as Pa nodded at her

side, his eyes shining bright. 'What I was about to say is, those months when I went missing, girls,' she looked at Eliza and Angeline, 'there was a very good reason for it, which I can now explain. It was because I was going to see a solicitor to conduct some business. From today, I am now the new owner of The Silver Kettle tea room!'

Angeline gasped and then a slow smile spread across her face. She loved that place.

'And I'd like you to help me there, and you too, Eliza?'

Both girls looked at one another in awe and then turned to face Mrs Featherstone, nodding eagerly.

Tommy, Billy, Eddie and Reggie grinned.

'Always knew you had it in you, Ma!' Billy exclaimed.

'But where did you get the money from, Ma?' Tommy frowned.

'Your father left a little behind after he passed away. This coster business has always done quite well. I was able to place a deposit on the tea room earlier this year. My plan is now to sell this house and move us all into the rooms above The Silver Kettle. There's adequate room there for all of us including your family, Bert,' she smiled. 'That's if you don't mind sharing, kids? I thought Michael could share with Sammy, Angeline with Joanna, and my boys have always had to share a room.'

'What about you and Albert though?' asked Billy.

'There's another small room we can use after

we're wed of course.' Mrs Featherstone's cheeks flushed a pale pink, then glancing at Eliza as if she didn't want to leave her out, she said, 'I know you are all right at George's parents' house, but you'll always be welcome at ours. Well, hopefully, we'll see a lot of you anyway serving at the tea room.'

For a moment, Eliza looked a bit sad but she nodded and forced a smile.

'I know what you're thinking, that I won't continue with the sewing business? But that won't be true. My plan is once we get the tea room up and running, I'll employ more staff. There's an ideal room downstairs just behind the tea room itself, I'd like to turn it into a sewing room, so don't fret none.'

Now Eliza was beaming. 'You might have to wait a little bit longer for me to work there, though...' she said looking at her father.

'What's going on, darlin'?' Pa was looking worried now.

'Nothing to get upset about, in fact, quite the opposite. I'm going to have a baby!'

'Oh, my goodness, how lovely!' exclaimed Mrs Featherstone. 'This is a day for surprises!'

'When is it due?' asked Pa, as he wiped away a tear with the back of his hand.

'Sometime next June.'

'That's fantastic news!' He hugged her close to his chest.

'Well done, our Eliza!' said Michael as he patted her on the shoulder.

'I think this is time for a celebration!' Mrs Featherstone looked around at everyone. 'Angeline, could you please fetch the mince pies I've laid out on a tray, from the scullery? And Bertie, please could you pour that sherry on the table over there?'

Both nodded at her.

And as everyone raised a glass to toast the good news, Angeline glanced out of the window, high above the cellar steps. It had started to snow.

'Merry Christmas, all!' Pa said as he raised his glass above his head and everyone, except the little ones who were drinking cups of milk, raised their glasses too.

'Yes, God Bless us all!' said Angeline as a tear of happiness slipped down her cheek, finding its way into her glass of sherry.

This Christmas was going to be a good one for everyone concerned. And as she pictured the beautiful angel doll sat on her bedside cabinet back home, she wondered if it somehow symbolised peace, joy and unity for her family once again. But the greatest gift they'd all been given this Christmas, was the gift of love.

About The Author

Lynette Rees

"My favourite author - this lady has just overtaken Catherine Cookson - I can't wait to read more!" ~ Amazon Reviewer

Lynette Rees lives in Wales and has been writing since she was a child. She's in the fortunate position of being a hybrid author - as well as independently publishing some of her novels, she's also published with Quercus Books/Hachette UK. Currently, her most popular novels with readers are: The Widow of Wakeford, Ada the Coster Girl, Black Diamonds and The Ragged Urchin.

The Winter Waif, the story of one young girl's struggle to overcome adversity following the death of her mother, will be published by Boldwood Books in January 2024. This will be followed by two other titles focusing on the lives of another two children growing up in the bustling

Welsh town of Merthyr Tydfl where the ironworks and coalpits are the main industries and a life of hardship is the norm.

Lynette enjoys the freedom of writing in a variety of genres including: crime fiction and contemporary romance, though her first love is historical fiction which complements her interest in local history and genealogy. When she's not writing, or even when she is writing, Lynette enjoys a glass of wine and the odd piece of chocolate as she creates stories where the characters guide her hand. She honestly has no idea how a story will turn out until the characters tell their own tales in their own unique ways.

The most important thing to Lynette is her family and her stories illustrate this with their warm characters who often show a great deal of compassion for others and the plight they find themselves in.

Praise for Lynette Rees:

The Matchgirl: "Beautifully written and imagined, this is both an entertaining story and a fascinating slice of life-changing history..." - book review - The Lancashire Post

Beneath a Sicilian Sun (retitled: Seduced by the Sicilian): "I was seeing everything described in this. This story is also very emotional and touching with everything that happens. The emotions that they feel are expressed beautifully..." - Sanfrancisco Review of Books

Printed in Great Britain
by Amazon